Musée d'art et d'histoire du Judaïsme

The Musée d'art et d'histoire du Judaïsme was inaugurated on Monday 30 November 1998 by President Jacques Chirac.

President
THÉO KLEIN

Director and Chief-Curator
LAURENCE SIGAL-KLAGSBALD

Numerous donors have given their support to help build up the collection of the Musée d'art et d'histoire du Judaïsme, in particular:
Captain Dreyfus'grandchildren and family, Mrs Claire Maratier, Mr. Georges Aboucaya, the late Ruben Lipchitz, who donated a substantial body of works, the Kraemer family, Mr. Christian Boltanski, as well as the Amado family, Mrs Sete Guetta, Mrs Lydie Lachenal, the Nahmias family, Mr. Victor Klagsbald, Mr. Théo Klein, Mr. Daniel Meyer and the Nordmann family.
The Museum also wishes to thank all those who, for fifty years, helped build up the collections of the Musée d'Art juif de Paris.

Liberté • Égalité • Fraternité
RÉPUBLIQUE FRANÇAISE

Ministère Culture Communication

MAIRIE DE PARIS

Contents

The Musée d'art et d'histoire du Judaïsme

The Musée d'art et d'histoire du Judaïsme aims to present Jewish culture in its immediacy and to explore its specific forms. Our approach is based on models drawn from within the Jewish intellectual, spiritual and social framework. The Museum covers only the formation and development of Judaism, excluding from its remit anything that is not related to Judaism itself, at least in this initial stage.

A panorama of the artistic, visual and material heritage of the Jewish communities dispersed throughout the world cannot ignore fundamental questions, even if it is hard to define the essence of Judaism and account for its continuing survival. Is Judaism a religion, the history of a particular nation, or is it, what one might venture to call a culture or a civilisation? Although it was undeniably founded as a religion, and was the source of the great monotheistic religions, Judaism is not simply a theological doctrine; it is also the unique destiny of a people whose identity has been forged through the vicissitudes of its history.

In this respect, Jewish history forces us to reconsider the concept of nationhood to include an essential feature of the Jewish phenomenon: exile. This question lies at the heart of a genuine methodological difficulty encountered by historians. Is there a unity that transcends the diversity of the Jewish communities, their evolution in time and their geographical dispersion? Can the unique experience of the Jewish community be understood on the basis of a single concept embracing all the social, spiritual, intellectual and artistic phenomena, and establishing its cultural continuity in time and space?

To present a global history of Judaism is not within the scope or ambition of a museum, even if it does, inevitably, touch on countless debates that have been taking place since the nineteenth century. A museum has neither the freedom nor the discipline

Arch of Titus
Polidoro de Caravaggio
(b. 1492, Caravaggio, -
d. 1543, Messina)
Italy, 18th century
Pen and sepia wash on board
20.6 x 38.7 cm
Gift of Georges Aboucaya
in memory of
Colette Aboucaya-Spira
MAHJ 91.12.71

of history or the human sciences; the nature of its material is not knowledge or information, and, even when there is a philosophy underpinning the museology, the museum shows but does not speak; the remit of a history museum is even tougher than that of the historian, for it can only arrange the works that it possesses, without being able to develop a continuous thread.

The contemporary era leads us to re-examine this question of "being Jewish". For most Jews, the religious definition has given way to a secular identity but with a distinct consciousness which asserts itself in a culture whose boundaries are becoming increasingly nebulous. A defined territory with unshifting boundaries and a specific destiny no longer exists. To be Jewish at the close of the twentieth century is often to exercise a consciousness beyond Judaism as a system, to be part of historical events made up of crises and dramatic changes, and to experience a sometimes contradictory tension between a presence in the world and the search for a uniqueness with fading parameters.

The museum visit

The museum visit explores the various forms covered by the notion of Jewish art, and shows the wealth of resources it can bring to the knowledge of Jewish culture. By returning to the history of the Jewish communities in France, Europe and North Africa, it studies different aspects of the Jewish world. The aim is not to establish an exhaustive, consistent history of Israel, but to highlight specific moments in the development of the Jewish people in exile. The displays are based on the key events that have marked Judaism, from the settlement of Jewish communities in France and in Europe to the expulsion of the Jews from Spain and its consequences, from the political Emancipation of the Jews under the French Revolution until World War Two. The early period, from the origins of Israel to the end of Antiquity, is only mentioned in the introductory gallery; this is not deliberate, but simply reflects the content of the collections.

Breaking with the hitherto traditional format of Jewish museums or "Jewish galleries" in regional museums in France and Europe, the museum visit does not follow the phases of religious life, nor does it acknowledge a distinction between tradition on the

The Vision of the Prophet Ezekiel: the Resurrection of the Dead
Doura Europos Synagogue
244-245
Damascus National Museum

one hand, and history and identity on the other. We feel that such an approach isolates Judaism from its historic destiny, which evolved out of the relations between the communities and their environment, long before the profound changes associated with the Emancipation of the Jews in Europe.

The visit begins in the introductory gallery with a display of the enduring elements of Jewish society, fundamental texts and symbolic objects. Each subsequent gallery corresponds to a combination of an era, a geographical region and a theme. The displays are consistent in terms of provenance, providing the historical, social and cultural context of the exhibits.

The concept that guides the visitor through space and time is that of the passing and relocation of centres of Judaism. Moving from one gallery to another highlights the diversity of social and cultural models. They are not evoked as a phenomenon experienced, but as being, at least in part, the fruit of Judaism's constructive way of thinking and being. The visit also puts the emphasis on the importance of social, economic and intellectual networks which partly compensate for the dispersion and scattering of Jewish communities

Jewish Art

The Museum's approach to the complex definition of Jewish art was to divide it into historical periods. The art of the modern era cannot be viewed in the same way as that of Antiquity, when the Children of Israel lived in the Promised Land steeped in holiness. The displays highlight phases in the development of Jewish art and establish that it has many different facets.

This approach makes it possible to challenge the rigid interpretation that the second commandment forbidding any likenesses of God or of His creatures (Exodus 20:4-6), automatically precluded Judaism from artistic creation. Major examples dating from the first centuries, such as the frescos from the synagogue of Doura Europos in Syria and the mosaics from the synagogues of Galilee show that this is certainly not the case.

The role of art in Jewish civilisation is bound up with a number of specific factors. Vestiges of Jewish art over a long period extending from the Middle Ages to the beginning of the nineteenth century mostly reveal the predominance of the religious content. The collections that form the core of the museum show that Jewish art developed chiefly in synagogue architecture and in the applied arts. Rabbinical Judaism undeniably encouraged the transfer of an aesthetic preoccupation to handicrafts, with the emphasis on the purpose of the object – the glorification of God through the embellishment of ritual instruments – as opposed to artistic creation. This concept of Jewish art defines it by its function, form and decoration and often by its author or sponsor.

This legacy is mainly made up of objects used for synagogue worship, and to decorate the Torah – the scroll of parchment on which the books of the Pentateuch are written – and of the many items used in day-to-day Jewish practice: objects used in worship, Sabbath lights, ceremonial drinking cups, lamps for the festival of *Hanukkah*, ritual garments, amulets and everyday objects. These objects, diverse in form and style, demonstrate a creativity sustained by an extraordinarily rich decorative and symbolic iconography. They illustrate the importance of tradition, the organisation of the community, of language and the written word as means of cementing communities. But, influenced also by the artistic trends in which they were born, they embody the interaction between a particular system of reference and the surrounding civilisations.

A second period, covering the years from the 1840s to the turn of the century, produced a generation of Jewish painters who had access to the schools of fine arts as a result of Emancipation. These artists still took a thematic approach, expressing themselves through genre painting. In Germany and France, they devoted themselves to the depiction of solemn or intimate moments of Jewish life. Painters emerged across Europe who all helped immortalise images of the traditional world: in Austria, Isidor Kaufmann; in Poland, Samuel Hirszenberg, Leopold Pilichovsky and Maurycy Trembacz; in Russia, Yehudah Penn, Chagall's first master.

Echoing the historical debates on the future of Judaism in the West which arose at the beginning of the twentieth century, artists explored a whole range of aesthetic options. The Russians, such as El Lissitzky, Nathan Altman, Issachar Rybak and, of course,

Marc Chagall, found their inspiration for an authentic Jewish art in folk art and decoration which expressed itself mainly in graphic art. In Berlin, questions of national identity and Zionism prompted artists to draw on the Orient of biblical times, to the Jugendstil and Expressionist movements, and were extended into the area of typography. Demonstrating the close link between artistic tendencies and contemporary intellectual and political movements, the main exponents of this trend, Ephraim Moses Lilien, Jakob Steinhardt and Joseph Budko emigrated to Palestine.

This experimentation indicated a new attitude which was reflected in the Jewish avant-garde literary and artistic movements in Warsaw. These artists were not concerned with taking the disappearing Jewish way of life as their theme, or with depicting Jews, but were attempting to link the old and the new and to find specific forms of expression. Underlying the question of themes and style, which varied greatly and encompassed all the turn-of-the-century artistic movements, was the exploration of the identity of Jewish art.

This quest for an "idea" whereby all spheres of Jewish life, all aspects of Jewish civilisation and all forms of expression would find cohesion comes to an end at this point. We are now on slippery ground where there is no longer a system of references, a closed world or a theory: the artist abandons a cultural register and ethnicity. Through the language of art, the museum explores paths, sometimes based on theory, sometimes random, taken by artists who, each following their own route, have experienced this radical reshaping of modern Jewish identity resulting from Emancipation and the tragic upheavals that shattered the twentieth century.

History of the collections

The Musée d'art et d'histoire du Judaïsme is the successor to the Musée d'art juif de Paris, established in 1948 by a private association to pay homage to a culture that had been destroyed by the Holocaust. The first collections of this museum comprised religious objects handed back in 1951 by the American Jewish Restitution Successor Organisation, commissioned to redistribute Jewish cultural goods looted by the Nazis. Then, on the initiative of the museum's founder, Léon Frenkiel, a collection of documents on European synagogue architecture was built up. In the early years, acquisitions consisted mainly of European religious objects and also sought to represent North African Judaism. Then, the museum's first curator, Marie Chabchay, embarked on building up a narrow but comprehensive collection of graphic works by Russian and German Jewish artists. There followed works by artists from the Paris school, and then, more recently, various gifts. Sophie Rosenberg succeeded Marie Chabchay, and was in charge of the museum from 1975 to 1998, also contributing to the enhancement of the collection.

The other core collection comes from the Musée national du Moyen Âge. This collection, which played a key role in gaining recognition for Jewish art, was built up by Isaac Strauss, a Jew of Alsatian origin, born in Strasbourg in 1806, who moved to Paris in 1827. Appointed by Louis-Philippe to supervise Court balls, then music director of the Vichy spa establishment, he retained these responsibilities under the Second Empire. His villa at Vichy housed a large collection of furniture and works of art.

Marie Chabchay
Paris, early 20th century
Photograph by
Michael Nappelbaum

Ary Scheffer
(b. 1795, Dordrecht, -
d. 1858, Argenteuil,)
Charlotte de Rothschild
(1825-1889)
1836, Oil on canvas
Private collection, France

During his travels throughout Europe, he acquired items of furniture, ceremonial objects and Hebrew manuscripts, building up a pioneering collection of outstanding quality.

This collection was featured in the Universal Exhibition of 1878 at the Palais du Trocadéro, and this had a decisive impact on the formation of large Jewish collections at the end of the nineteenth century. The objects were described by Georges Stenne in a catalogue which included very clear sketches, and this was the first bibliographical reference to Jewish art.

At the time of his death, Strauss's collection of Jewish objects amounted to a hundred and forty nine pieces. After changing hands a number of times, it was acquired in 1890 by Baroness Nathaniel de Rothschild who gave it to the State, and it was subsequently augmented by individual gifts. However, the apparent eclecticism of this collection, which contains some remarkable and unique pieces, shows a complete indifference to history and folk tradition.

From conception to completion

The idea of setting up a new museum to house these two collections was mooted in 1980 and was in keeping with the wishes of the Musée d'art juif, expressed by the founders and its president, Claude-Gérard Marcus, who wanted to expand the existing museum. There was a dazzling demonstration of the new museum's potential in 1981 with the exhibition of the Strauss collection at the Grand Palais and the publication of a *Catalogue raisonné*, written by Victor Klagsbald.

Jacques Chirac, mayor of Paris at the time, offered the Hôtel de Saint-Aignan as the site for the planned museum.
The project received the support of the Ministry of Culture. Steered by Théo Klein, then President of the Representative Council of Jewish Institutions in France, negotiations with the main Jewish Institutions culminated in an agreement signed in 1986 between Jacques Chirac and Minister for Culture, Jack Lang.

The Musée d'art et d'histoire du Judaïsme is administered by an association established in 1988, comprising representatives from the Ministry of Culture and Communication, the City of Paris, and the chief institutions of the French Jewish community. The President of the association is Claude-Gérard Marcus, seconded by Vice-President Théo Klein.

The budget for the restoration and refurbishment of the building and the operating costs are shared between the Ministry of Culture and Communication and the City of Paris.

The long-term loans from the Musée d'Art juif and the Musée national du Moyen Âge have been augmented by loans from the Musée National d'Art moderne – Centre Georges Pompidou, the Musée du Louvre, the Musée d'Orsay, the Musée national des Arts d'Afrique et d'Océanie. The collection of ceremonial art has been enriched by works from the treasure-house of the Paris synagogues loaned by the Consistories of Paris, of liturgical textiles by the Jewish Museum of Prague, and a collection of folk art objects from the Musée historique lorrain, in Nancy. The Fondation du judaïsme français has contributed several modern and contemporary works of art, and the Carnavalet museum has added to the collection of medieval tombstones.

LAURENCE SIGAL-KLAGSBALD

Jewish ceremonial objects
17th and 18th centuries
As displayed at the turn of the century in a display case of the Musée national du Moyen Âge, in Paris.

The Hôtel de Saint-Aignan

The Hôtel d'Avaux (1644-1650)

The mansion was built by Claude de Mesmes, the Count of Avaux, who served under Richelieu and Mazarin and was instrumental in negotiating the Peace of Westphalia in 1648. The plans were drawn up by architect Pierre Le Muet, who owed his reputation to a work he had published in 1623, *Manière de bâtir pour toutes sortes de personnes* (How to Build for Every Kind of Person), and to the castles he had constructed at Pont-sur-Seine and Chavigny in Touraine, and Tanlay in Burgundy, between 1638 and 1645.

The site of the residence was the large, irregular-shaped plot of land on which stood the family home inherited by Claude d'Avaux in 1642. Having knocked down the existing building, Le Muet adopted the customary layout for large aristocratic residences, the main building set back from the street, across a large, virtually rectangular courtyard, that on entering looks square, with one wing branching off to the right (kitchen, servants' hall and dining room on the ground floor, large gallery on the first floor, like the early design of the Hôtel de Sully). A corridor led to the little farmyard with sheds and stables, and an entrance direct from the street. On the left, Le Muet constructed a party wall in the same place as the one built by Philippe Auguste. Its symmetrical design reflected the right wing, with pilasters and imitation windows, creating a bogus wall.

Paul de Beauvillier, Duke of Saint-Aignan, who bought the mansion in 1688, had the gallery converted to apartments, and, leading up to them, a staircase partly overhanging the little courtyard. He used a small adjoining piece of land, purchased from a neighbour, to extend the right wing into the garden, and installed little apartments in it. He had the garden re-landscaped by André Le Nôtre creating a flowerbed, pool and trellis.

Confiscated in 1792, the mansion became the headquarters of the seventh municipality in 1795, then of the seventh

Main courtyard

arrondissement until 1823, before being divided into commercial premises of all kinds, which resulted in the building being split into different levels and raised, and the addition of other features.
It was purchased in 1962 by the City of Paris, and listed as a historic monument in 1963. Renovation work took more than twenty-five years, with long periods of interruption. Apart from one or two 1690 additions, and with a few errors, (dormers on the courtyard side, ceiling of the first floor lower than the arches of the windows), the restoration works and some of the reconstruction (roofing, staircase), completed in 1998, reinstated the original mansion, restoring to French art one of the finest examples of classical Parisian architecture dating back to the regency of Anne of Austria.

The grand staircase

The Italian architect Vincenzo Scamozzi, who travelled to France at the beginning of the seventeenth century, was amazed that one entered via the stairway, even in large houses. The Hôtel de Sully still has this feature, but around 1640, the use of the hall, hitherto rare, became increasingly common. Here, as in the Château de Maisons, a hall, given noble treatment in the classical style, with niches and pilasters, leads to the staircase.

But, although the nineteenth-century alterations left the hall intact, the staircase was completely destroyed. Only archaeological traces remained (notches on the walls of the stairwell where the steps used to be, the ripping out of the vaults supporting the landings, balusters and fragments of the stringer). With the help of Le Muet's plans, it was possible to reproduce the staircase, giving a clear idea of the original.

It was based on the staircase in the château at Maisons designed by François Mansart, itself a smaller version of the spectacular but unfinished one he had built at Blois. The staircase only goes up to the first floor, and the second floor is reached by a small staircase placed to one side. The upper landing encircles the stairwell around an oval opening, making it possible to see the calotte, the caplike vault, from below.

The *trompe l'œil* perspective on the calotte – in fact the only *quadratura*, excluding the stage – is a modern creation based on a sketch for the Hôtel d'Avaux. The original sketch however bears

Opposite page
The hall, view of the grand staircase

the explicit annotation "*poin fait*" (not done). Reinstating it is perhaps contrary to Claude d'Avaux's decision and Le Muet's ultimate choice to leave the calotte white.

The dining room

Around 1640, the dining room came into widespread use in large Parisian town houses. Here, the architect Le Muet skilfully places it in the wing at an angle, close to the kitchen, but separated from the service rooms by the corridor that leads to the farmyard.

The room was decorated in *grisaille*, which can be dated back to the initial works, around 1650. This décor, which is not mentioned in any of the old Paris guide books, had been forgotten and painted over. During the first restoration programme, it remained undiscovered, and was further damaged. Revealed during the second, more painstaking restoration effort, fragments of it have re-emerged: the symmetrical arrangement of the motifs enables us to reconstitute it almost entirely on paper, but a complete restoration would ruin the original.

No details of any commission have been found, but the style, which clearly evokes that of the Romans, is reminiscent of the *grisaille* décor of the gallery of the Château de Tanlay, painted in 1646 by Rémy Vuibert (1600-1652), under the supervision of Le Muet. Like Tanlay, this complex is one of the finest examples of the serene classicism now known as "Atticism". The taste for classical figures and ornaments, light or monochrome paint, balanced compositions and figures in garments with pleated drapery was prevalent in Paris in the 1640s, after Poussin's stay. Rémy Vuibert was one of the key exponents of this style.

CLAUDE MIGNOT
University of Tours

**The restoration of the building was carried out under the supervision of Bernard Fonquernie, chief architect, Historic Monuments.
The interior design and displays are the work of Catherine Bizouard and François Pin, in association with Lean Mai.**

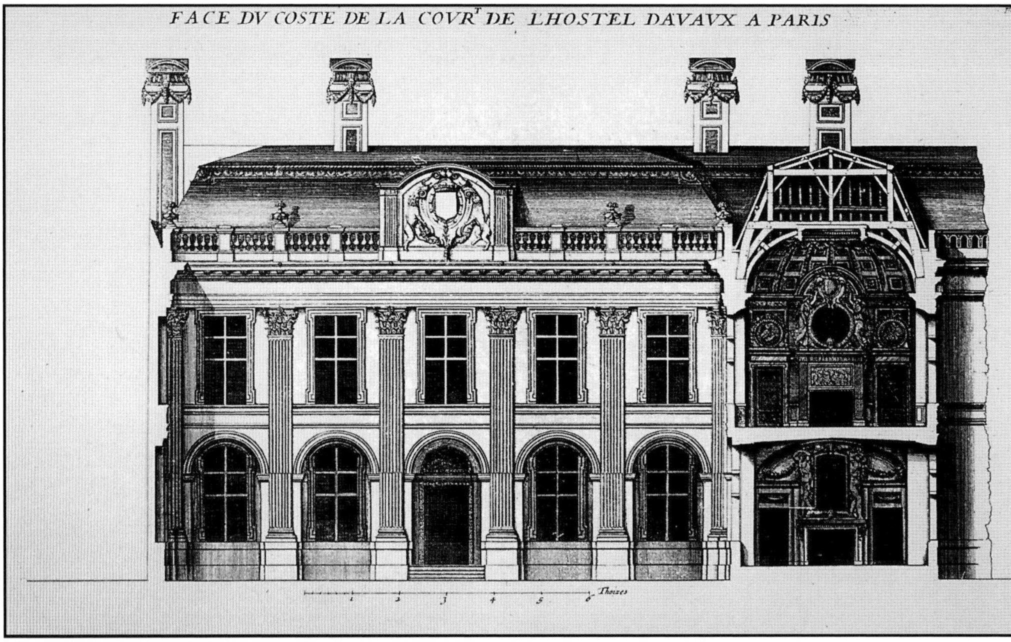

Pierre Le Muet
Plans for the façade overlooking the courtyard of the Hôtel d'Avaux
Engraved cross-section by Jean Marot, 1647.

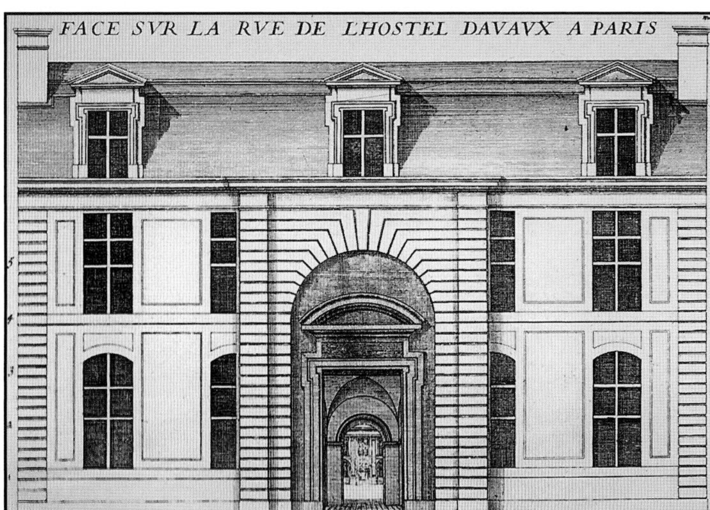

Pierre Le Muet
Plans for the façade overlooking the street
Engraved cross-section by Jean Marot, 1647.

1 Introductory Gallery

Jewish history goes back thousands of years, and its continuity is extraordinary given the dispersal of the Jewish people. The Introductory Gallery is designed to present the most important landmarks in this uninterrupted history, the moments which have guaranteed it a place in the history of nations. Starting with the Covenant with Abraham, the destiny of Israel evolved between the Exodus from Egypt, the revelation on Mount Sinai and the arrival of the Hebrews in the Land of Canaan. But from earliest Antiquity, the political practice of the Jewish people as a sovereign nation has been governed by the atypical experience of exile. Jewish identity has consequently been a delicate compromise between upholding independent values and adapting to surroundings.

The Introductory Gallery presents a large number of religious and secular texts, some poetic, painted in fresco, which illustrate the permanence of the Hebrew language, from its birth to the twentieth century, and the predominance of the written word in the Jewish civilisation. The display is built around symbolic objects representing the main vectors of Judaism's cohesion.

Abraham's Covenant, bound up with the birth of the Hebrew people and their relation to the Promised Land, is illustrated by Genesis 12: 1-3 and 17: 2-11. A procession of faces, some anonymous, some famous, from Antiquity to the present day, shows the diversity of the Jewish people. A model of Jerusalem reflects the Jews' ties with that city, echoed in an elegy to Zion by Yehudah Halevi, a twelfth-century Spanish poet. The idea of revealed religion is embodied by the parchment scrolls inscribed with the text of the Torah, the fundamental spiritual source and legal authority of Jewish tradition. As the transmission of Judaism relies as much on ritual as on teaching, and traditional worship is symbolised here by a *Hanukkah* lamp, with its many associations relating to the religious and political sovereignty of the Jewish people, as well as being part of religious ritual.

Torah Scroll
Sefer Torah
Italy or Ottoman Empire, 16th century?
Black ink on parchment
H. 45.5 cm
Private collection
D.974.2

Hanukkah lamp
Johann Michael Schüler
(Frankfurt-on-Main, 1658-1718)
Chased and engraved silver
Strauss collection,
Rothschild donation
On long-term loan
from the Musée national
du Moyen Âge, Paris
D.98.4.26

Torah ornaments
Rimmonim
Shanghai, 19th century
Cast and pierced silver
31.5 x 12 cm
Gift of Abraham Benchetrit
to the Synagogue of rue Buffault
On long-term loan
from the Paris Consistory
D.96.2.9.1-2

Relief map of Jerusalem
Odessa, 1892
Gilded wood, card, paper mâché
and glass beads
131 x 138 x 27 cm
Gift of David Kauffmann
Gift of the Musée d'Art juif
de Paris
MAHJ 2002.1.273

Exile is a determining aspect of the Jewish historical experience; its specific character derives from overcoming the pain of loss by interacting with the surrounding civilisations, and these have left their mark on all spheres of Jewish society and culture. Typical of this reciprocal influence is a pair of Torah finials in the form of Pagodas, made in Shanghai at the end of the nineteenth century. Lastly, the french revolutionary decree granting the Jews civil rights marks the beginning of the period of emancipation. This events-led approach culminates in a sculpture by Chana Orloff entitled *Le Peintre juif* (the Jewish painter), which expresses the permanent questioning of modern Jewish identity. This portrayal of a thinker contravenes the Jewish prohibition against portraying the human form in art, and paves the way for the debate on the future of a Jewish art. The dramatic upheavals of the twentieth century are reflected in the poem by H̲ayyim Nah̲man Bialik, *In the City of Slaughter*, which forms the last milestone ending this representation of the essence of Judaism.

Decree granting the emancipation of the Jews of the Portugal, Spain and Avignon
Paris, 1790
Printed (3 pages)
24 x 18.5 cm
MAHJ 91.1.1

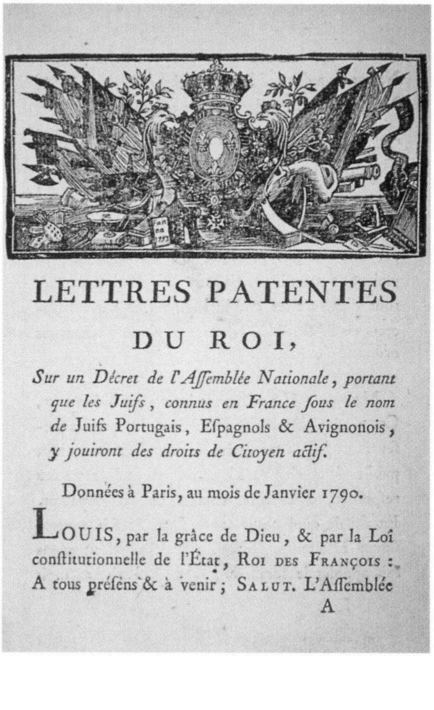

LETTRES PATENTES

DU ROI,

Sur un Décret de l'Aſſemblée Nationale, portant que les Juifs, connus en France ſous le nom de Juifs Portugais, Eſpagnols & Avignonois, *y jouiront des droits de Citoyen actif.*

Données à Paris, au mois de Janvier 1790.

LOUIS, par la grâce de Dieu, & par la Loi conſtitutionnelle de l'État, ROI DES FRANÇOIS : A tous préſens & à venir ; SALUT. L'Aſſemblée

A

Chana Orloff
(b. 1888, Tsara Konstantinovska -
d. 1968, Tel Aviv)
The Jewish painter, Reisin?
Paris, 1920
Bronze
38.2 x 21.3 x 26.2 cm
Gift of the Justman-Tamir family
MAHJ 98.6.1

French Jewry in the Middle Ages

2

***Hanukkah* lamp**
France, 14th century
Bronze
15.5 x 14.7 cm
Strauss Collection,
Rothschild donation
On long-term loan
from the Musée national
du Moyen Âge, Paris
D. 98.4.17

Discovered in the 19th century in the old Jewish quarter of Lyon, this lamp dates back to pre-1394, the year of the last expulsion of the Jews from France. It is one of the oldest known objects of worship in the home from the Medieval period. Designed to be suspended from the wall, this lamp takes its inspiration from Gothic architecture, and its triangular shape is characteristic of the period.

Jewish communities can be traced back to the early centuries of the Christian era in Mediterranean Gaul, the Garonne valley and along the Rhône-Rhine axis.

The development of the Jewish communities was not hindered by the spread of Christianity in Gaul. However, with the baptism of Clovis in 496, Christianity became the official religion of the kingdom, and the Church dignitaries tried to divest Christian worship of all allusions to its Jewish origins. While the Merovingian period, from the fifth to the eighth century, saw the decline of the Jewish community, the Jews flourished once again under Charlemagne in the ninth and tenth centuries. They continued to thrive throughout the Middle Ages, in two main areas: Provence and Languedoc, and also in the area encompassing northern and eastern France. Jews had access to all the professions and played a major role in trade between East and West. However, they were barred from having Christian slaves. After the collapse of the Carolingian empire in 843 the status of Jews varied according to whether they lived in the principalities, *seigneuries* or on the property of the King of France, the *Domaine Royal*. Some regions offered the Jewish communities favourable conditions, and thriving communities developed north of the Loire, in this area which bears the name of *Tsarfat*. In Champagne in the eleventh century, Rashi of Troyes founded a famous Talmud school.

But at the instigation of the clergy, the Jews became increasingly linked to the Antichrist, and were viewed with suspicion, even hostility. The first crusade in 1096, which caused much less bloodshed in France than in the Rhineland, nevertheless sparked outbursts of violence against Jewish homes in Metz and Rouen. This period promoted the growth of Christian hostility towards the Jews. Accused of spreading epidemics, defiling the Host, and poisoning wells and rivers, the Jews – alluded to through the allegory of the blindfolded synagogue – were demonised as the evil agents of Christian misfortune. The first accusation of ritual murder in France was made in 1171, in Blois, where thirty-two Jews were burned.

The thirteenth century saw the beginning of a period of great insecurity for French Jews: the Church's offensive, with the strong backing of the secular authorities, became more virulent. The Fourth Lateran Council, convened by Pope Innocent III in 1215, brought together nearly 5,000 priests determined to mark symbolically the power of Christianity over the West. They stressed the need to identify the Jews immediately, the better to exclude them.

Consequently, in 1227, the Council of Narbonne made it compulsory for Jews to wear a distinguishing badge. In 1269, Louis IX (Saint Louis) decreed that French Jews must wear a *rouelle*, a round piece of fabric, sewn onto their clothing, in the centre of the chest, making them easy prey for mass loathing, encouraged by the clergy.

The territorial expansion of the Capetian kingdom and the establishment of a central administration signalled an important change for the Jewish communities of France. There were more restrictions and exclusions, and, barred from owning property, the Jews found themselves confined to the money-lending professions. Regarded as serfs belonging to the Royal Treasury, they were used as sources of revenue. Keen to confiscate some of their wealth, Philippe Auguste expelled the Jews from the kingdom in 1188, but called them back in 1198. In 1306, Philip IV, known as Philip the Fair, decreed the expulsion of the kingdom's 100,000 Jews. This pattern of expulsions and repeals, chiefly motivated by economic dictates, continued during the reigns of his successors, destroying all forms of community life. Charles VI's edict of 1394 expelling all the Jews from France was the final blow for a population that was already greatly diminished.

In Provence, which was separate from the kingdom of France, the Jewish communities of Marseille, Narbonne and Lunel thrived in the thirteenth century, in sharp contrast to this decline. The Jews were profoundly affected by the "*Croisade des Pastoureaux*" (Shepherds' Crusade) and the persecutions following the Black Death of 1348. Provence became part of the Kingdom of France in 1481, expelling the Jews in 1498, following the French example and thus joining a vast Europe-wide movement.

Rashi and the Tossafists

The work of Rashi of Troyes (1040–1105) is the most outstanding example of the vitality of the Jewish communities north of the Loire. Through his teachings and his commentaries on the Bible and the Talmud, Rashi exercised a profound influence not only over Jewish spiritual life, but also on Christian theologians. In engaging in discussions on his commentary of the Talmud (*kunteres*) and in comparing Talmudic sources, his disciples, the Tossafists, composed *tossafot* (glosses) to Rashi's interpretations and conclusions, helping extend the influence of his work as far as the Orient.

The ibn Tibbon family

The ibn Tibbon family settled in the south of France in the twelfth century after the Almohads came to power in Spain. They played a vital role in the transfer of philosophical and scientific knowledge from the Orient to the West, by translating and disseminating works written in Arabic by Jewish and Muslim scholars. Translators, linguists and grammarians, Judah ibn Tibbon (c. 1120-c. 1190), and his son Samuel helped enrich the Hebrew language. From the twelfth century, the Hebrew of the Tibbons had a considerable impact and was widely disseminated, to the extent that it was adopted by all men of learning, whether they were Kabbalists, grammarians or Biblical exegetes.

Prayer Book for the Year, *Mahzor*
Rhineland, 1312-1313
Parchment, morocco-bound
23 x 15.8 cm
Strauss collection,
Rothschild donation
On long-term loan
from the Musée national
du Moyen Âge, Paris
D.98.4.28

This manuscript includes a calendar beginning in the year 1312 or 1313, making it possible to date it. The script and the date the book was produced are very close to that of the expulsion of the Jews from France by Philippe the Fair in 1306, making it highly probable that it is the work of French scribes who had taken refuge in Rhineland. Evidence of the book's French origin can be found in the prayers which are those of the French communities, in the inclusion of liturgical poems – *piyyutim* – which are only known through the *Vitry Mahzor*, as well as in the use of old French terms transcribed into Hebrew. It contains the daily prayers, those of *Shabbat* and the Festivals, of *Pesah* with the *Haggadah*, the portions of the Torah – *parashot* – and the prayers for the New Moon.

Jewish cemeteries in Paris

During the Middle Ages, Parisian Jews built their cemeteries outside the residential districts, as required by Jewish custom. The biggest one was in use until the expulsion of the Jews by Philip the Fair in 1306. It lay between the former rue de la Harpe (now Boulevard St Michel), rue Pierre-Sarrazin, rue Hautefeuille and rue des Deux-Portes (now Boulevard St Germain). The remains came to light in 1849, when work began on the foundations for the Hachette publishing house. Not a single gravestone has survived from a second cemetery, used until 1273, and located between rue Galande and rue du Plâtre (now rue Domot). The existence of a third cemetery, east of rue des Juifs, now rue Ferdinand-Duval, was recently confirmed by the discovery of a splendid tombstone carved in 1364.

Tombstone
Paris, 1281
Limestone
113 x 55.5 x 10 cm
On long-term loan
from the Musée national
du Moyen Âge, Paris
CL.19401

In accordance with Ashkenazi custom, the tombstones from the Paris cemeteries stood upright over individual graves. This tombstone, bearing the date 1281, was found in 1849 at the site of the former cemetery located between rue Pierre-Sarrazin and rue de la Harpe. The epitaph is in Hebrew, and, following the traditional sequence, gives the rabbinical titles of two Parisian teachers: "This is the tombstone of our teacher Rabbi Salomon, son of our teacher Rabbi Judah, who departed for the Garden of Eden on the day of *Shabbat Korah* in the year 5041 of the calendar, may his memory live for ever in the world to come, may his soul be bound up with the living."

The expulsion of the Jews from Spain

On 31 March 1492, in Granada, the Catholic Monarchs, Ferdinand and Isabella, signed the edict expelling the Jews from Castile and Aragon, thus putting a brutal end to a Jewish presence that had lasted for more than a thousand years. Although it named the Jews, the edict was aimed especially at the *conversos*, or new Christians – Jews who had converted – and their descendants.

The edict stated that not enough "remedies" had been adopted to counter contacts between Jews and *conversos*: separate residential areas, the expulsion of the Jews of Andalusia in 1483, and the setting up of the Inquisition – between 1481 and 1492, the Inquisition tribunals tried around 13,000 new Christians, more than 1,000 of whom were sentenced to be burned at the stake. The expulsion in 1492 was the culmination of a decade-long internal process of marginalisation and expulsion.

The edict enjoined the Jews either to convert, or to leave Spanish soil before the end of July 1492, on pain of death. They were forced to sell their goods for derisory prices and were forbidden to take gold, silver or any other items of value with them. Given short notice, they were stripped of their possessions which further added to the horrors of the expulsion.

The exiles set sail for the Ottoman Empire, North Africa, or Italy; others made for Navarre and Provence, but most chose Portugal, which expelled them in 1497. King Manuel used violence and extreme cruelty to force them to convert. The Kingdom of Navarre in turn expelled the Jews in 1498. These successive expulsions led to a vast transfer of culture and people, resulting in a profound Hispanisation of the Mediterranean Jewish world.

Alm box for the festival of *Purim*
Spain, 1319
Carved stone
13.2 x 12.5 cm
Gift of Alphonse de Rothschild
On long-term loan
from the Musée national
du Moyen Âge, Paris
D.98.4.87

This alm box is among the very rare surviving objects from before the expulsion of the Jews from Spain. It was used to collect donations to the synagogue during the festival of *Purim*. Tradition prescribes that on this day, people should give presents to their relatives and gifts to the poor (Esther 9:22). There are two inscriptions in Judeo-Spanish that make specific reference to the festival: *zekhirah del nes* (in remembrance of the miracle), in the medallion, and *Rey Ahasveros y la reyna Ester* (King Ahasuerus and Queen Esther). In fact, although no mention is made of divine intervention, the Talmud considers that "the deliverance of the Jews thanks to Esther was the last miracle" (*Yoma*, 29, a). The inscriptions are one of the oldest examples of the use of a language other than Hebrew or Aramaic on a ritual object.

The expulsion of the Jews from Spain

Prayer book
Moses ben Hayyim `Aqrish
Ferrara, 1512
Vellum, velvet
17.7 x 12.7 cm
Kann donation
On long-term loan
from the Musée national
du Moyen Âge, Paris
D.98.4.29

The contrast between the Sephardi lettering of this manuscript and its Italian-style decoration with frames filled with interlacing and foliage, rectangular fields and richly decorated medallions, shows the many influences encountered by the scribes who worked in several countries. In particular it reflects the itinerary of those who were expelled from Spain after 1492. Moses `Aqrish, known for other illuminated manuscripts, notes in the colophon that he is a refugee from Spain and that he completed this manuscript in Ferrara in 1512 (1 Adar 5272).

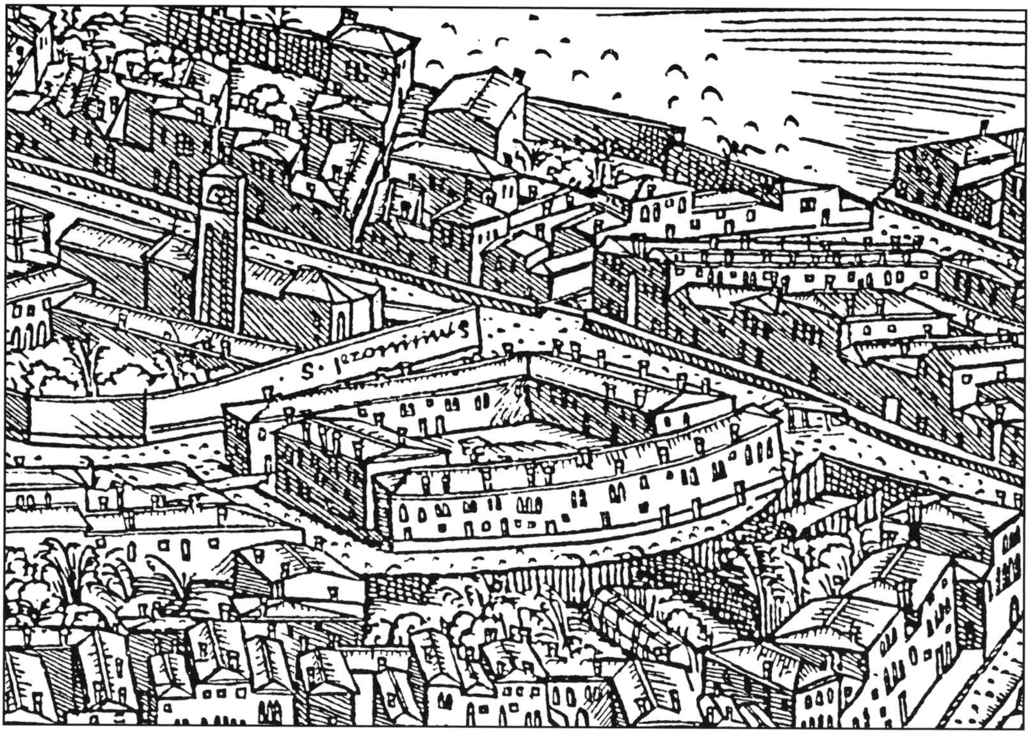
S. Ieronimus

3 Italian Jewry, from the Renaissance to the eighteenth century

From the end of the thirteenth century, the communes of central and northern Italy exerted a powerful attraction for the Jewish financiers of Rome and beyond the Alps. In fact, many Italian Jewish communities, some of which have survived until today, were established when Jewish merchants settled in these city republics. These men handled a lot of business in Rome, where they became indispensable to the Church authorities. Alone or in groups along the consular routes, they sometimes put down roots in places offering them adequate guarantees of security for their investments, a convenient tax regime, and contacts interested in the capital they had brought with them. Thus a tight network of tiny communities grew up in the centre of the peninsula, extending gradually as the migratory trend continued northwards.

In the second half of the fourteenth century, these Roman Jews reached the valley of the Po, at the same time as other Jewish merchants driven out of the Germanic countries by the wave of massacres triggered by the Black Death of 1348-1349. For them too, Italy seemed the logical place to seek refuge. The communes offered the fugitives relative security combined with interesting economic opportunities. Finally, the expulsion of the Jews from France by Charles VI in 1394 led to a third wave of Jewish merchants, fewer in number, who settled chiefly in Piedmont and Savoie.

These Jewish merchants and financiers were active throughout the period of the communes, in the thirteenth and fourteenth centuries. The Renaissance was a time of great prosperity for the Italian Jews. Their numbers had swollen to around 50,000, and the Jewish population was highly mobile. The Jews tended to be well-off – few made colossal fortunes, but there were not many poor – and well integrated into a surrounding society that bore the Jews astonishing goodwill. As always during the good times, the Italian Jews were actively involved in the general cultural creative output –

View of Venice, the Ghetto
Jacopo de Barbari
1500
Museo Civico Correr, Venice

Gracia Nassi the younger
Italy, 19th century minting
of a 16th-century medal
by Pastorino
Bronze
Diam. 6.5 cm
Strauss Collection,
Rothschild donation
On long-term loan
from the Musée national
du Moyen Âge, Paris
D.98.4.58

Gracia Nassi the younger was the niece of Gracia Nassi (Lisbon c. 1510 - Istanbul? Tiberias? 1569). Born into a Marrano family in Lisbon, Gracia Nassi found herself a widow and head of the Mendes family's banking empire. Banker to the kings of France and to Charles V, she returned to Judaism and devoted her energy and power to openly combating the Inquisition and protecting the Jews. In protest against the burning at the stake of twenty-six Marranos, she organised a blockade of the port of Ancona.

exemplified by the composer and theorist Salomone de' Rossi – as well as in specifically Jewish cultural activities.

The Renaissance spirit had a marked influence on Jewish studies in the Peninsula. This period saw the birth of a Jewish historiography (Azaria de' Rossi), an embryonic form of Jewish Biblical exegesis (Obadia ben Jacob Sforno, who also happened to be the Hebrew teacher of the German humanist Johannes Reuchlin), and a Jewish theatre (Leone d' Sommi Portaleone).

However, tolerant as it may have been, Italian society was Christian, by definition wary of the Jews and therefore potentially hostile. Already, Franciscan propaganda against usury, which was especially intense during the second half of the fifteenth century, led to the establishment throughout Italy of *montes pietatis*, charitable funds for the granting of interest-free loans secured by pledges to the poor.

This was an overt move to drive the Jews from the financial market, which they tended to dominate, partly because of the Church ban on Christian involvement, but above all as a result of their own social situation. Anti-Jewish feeling was simmering everywhere, and, in 1475, an accusation of ritual murder in Trento led to the extermination of the local Jewish community. This date is symbolic, marking the beginning of the period of confinement and expulsion for Italian Jewry. Furthermore, the expulsion of the Jews from Spain also had an impact on the fate of their fellow Jews in the Italian territories under Spanish domination. The era of tolerance was over.

The atmosphere became even more oppressive in the second half of the sixteenth century, when the Counter-Reformation, a vast enterprise to re-establish Roman Catholic control, sparked off the marginalisation of Italian Jews. The Jewish community, which had once played an active part in the social, economic and cultural life of the peninsula, was now no more than a cast of persecuted pariahs, as a result of the policies of the popes and princes of the Counter-Reformation.

The burning of the Talmud in 1553, the establishment of the Rome ghetto by Pope Paul IV in 1555 and the expulsion of the Jews from the pontifical states in 1569 were all spectacular events that were part of a process that had begun many years before and would continue for many more – in fact until the French entered Italy in 1796.

Synagogue Ark,
Aron ha-Kodesh
Modena, 1472
Carved and inlaid wood
265 x 130 x 78 cm
Strauss Collection,
Rothschild donation
On long-term loan
from the Musée national
du Moyen Âge, Paris
D.98.4.123

This piece, from the synagogue in Modena, is the only mediaeval Ashkenazi ark that has survived. Its two halves form a structure with a crenellated upper frieze reminiscent of the shape of a fortified tower, an allegory of the name of God as in the verse: "The name of the Lord is a tower of strength where the righteous may seek refuge." (Proverbs, 30:10). The painted inscriptions also evoke the religious and symbolic connection between the Ark and the Ark of the Covenant of the Temple of Jerusalem, both considered as the seat of divine presence.

The Synagogue

During their captivity in Babylon (586-538 BCE), the Jews were unable to worship in the Temple and so formed the habit of gathering together in an assembly (Greek: *sunagōgē*) of at least ten men (*minyan*) to pray and listen to the reading of the Torah. On their return from exile, this form of worship coexisted for several centuries with the Temple service. After the destruction of the second Temple in the year 70 CE, the synagogue became the centre of community life in the diaspora.

Although synagogue buildings vary according to local architectural influences, they all share a number of features. They must face east towards Jerusalem, and the interior is arranged around the two principal focuses of the service, the Ark (*Hekhal* or *Aron*) and the reading desk, the *Bimah*. Placed against the eastern wall and slightly raised by a few steps, is the Ark, containing several Torah Scrolls (*Sifrei Torah*). It is often decorated with an embroidered curtain (*Parokhet*).

Torah binder, *Mappah*
Cremona, 1582
Canvas lined with linen
14 x 330 cm
Strauss Collection,
Rothschild donation
On long-term loan
from the Musée national
du Moyen Âge, Paris
D.98.4.127

This binder, with a plant motif, is embroidered with verses from the Bible and a Hebrew text mentioning the name of the embroiderer, the wife of the donor: "[made] by his wife, lady Eve may she live! Daughter of the notable David Samuel Cohen, of holy memory, of Porto. She made this binder in honour of the Torah ..." The binders could also be cut from circumcision gowns, then embroidered by women in the family.

The Torah Ornaments

The synagogue service revolves around the *Sefer Torah*. The text is copied by the scribe onto a scroll made up of a series of parchments; each of the two extremities of the parchment is sewn to a wooden stave, called the Tree of Life (*Ets hayyim*). There are two categories of sacred objects: the first, the holy instruments (*Tashmishei Kedushah*), whose purpose is above all to protect the Torah from being tainted and to magnify it, as opposed to the second category, *Tashmishei Mitzvah*, all the objects associated with fulfilling the many commandments and ceremonies of Jewish life. Already in the Talmud there is reference to the silk fabrics encasing the scrolls. Once wrapped in a binder (*Mappah*), which keeps them rolled up, in Ashkenazi communities the scrolls are dressed in a mantle (*Me'il*), often richly ornamented, whereas in Oriental communities, they are locked in a cylindrical wooden case (*Tik*), painted or covered in silver ornaments. The Torah sometimes bears a crown (*Keter*), symbolising its supremacy (*Sayings of the Fathers* 4: 13), or the staves are ornamented with silver finials called *Rimmonim* (pomegranates) or *Tappuhim* (apples), in Sephardi communities, decorated with little bells that indicate the passage of the officiant. A decorative shield (*Tas*), into which little silver plates can be slipped for the various festivals, and the pointer (*Yad*) complete the ornaments.

The mantle, the plaque, the crown and the bells originate in the attire of the high priest and attest to the transfer of the notion of the sacred.

Liturgical mats
Italy, 18th century
Cotton satin,
silk thread, gold thread
Diam.: 61 cm
Strauss Collection,
Rothschild donation
On long-term loan
from the Musée national
du Moyen Âge, Paris
D.98.04.158-161

These mats, dedicated to the festivals of *Sukkot*, *Pesaẖ*, and *Rosh ha-Shana* (a fourth mat, not shown here, is dedicated to *Simẖat Torah*), were probably used to cover the Torah scroll between two readings. During these festivals, considered as days of judgment, clothes and synagogue ornaments had to be white, the colour associated with death and purity.

Circumcision chair
Northern Italy, late
17th century – early 18th century
Carved, gilded wood
150 x 66.5 x 53 cm
MAHJ 90.8.1

This circumcision chair belonged to an Italian synagogue. The circlet of the crown bears an Aramaic inscription mentioning the destination of the object: *Dein Qursaya de Eliyahu zakhur la-tov* (this is the chair of Elijah, whose memory is blessed). The prophet Elijah, described as the "angel of the Covenant" presides over the circumcision as protector of the newborn. Circumcision chairs have one or two seats – one for the godfather (*Sanddak*) and the other for the prophet. One-seated chairs are found more frequently in Sephardi and Italian communities. The mask of a faun adorning the struts is borrowed from mythology and the Italian decorative repertoire, which is not unusual in Jewish religious objects. This chair once belonged to Zadoc Kahn, chief rabbi of France from 1868 to 1905, and remained in his family.

The life Cycle

The life Cycle revolves around four key events: birth, *Bar Mitzvah*, marriage and death, which give the individual their place in the community.

Circumcision

Circumcision (*Brit Milah*) is the tangible sign of the covenant with God. It derives from the text of Genesis XVII, 9-13: "God said to Abraham ... Here is my covenant that you will keep between me and you and your descendants after you ... And he that is eight days old shall be circumcised among you every male ...."

A fundamental duty in Judaism, it is performed on the eighth day, in the presence of ten men, by a *Mohel*. The godfather (*Sanddak*) sits on one of the two chairs generally reserved for this ceremony. The other, called "the throne of Eliyah", is symbolically kept for the prophet who is invited, according to tradition, to every circumcision. At the end of the ritual, the father recites the benediction and names the child. The ritual concludes with a festive meal for all the guests (*Se'udat Mitzvah*).

A Jewish wedding
A circumcision
c. 1780
Attributed to Marco Marcuola
(Verona, 1740-Venice, 1793)
Oil on canvas
41.9 x 81 cm
Acquired in 1996 with
the support of the FRAM
Île-de-France
MAHJ 96.5.1 and 2

This pair of paintings depicts two scenes from Jewish life, a subject which inspired a number of 18th-century painters and etchers, particularly in Venice. The first shows a Jewish wedding which is taking place in a Venetian interior. Before the institution of synagogue weddings, in the 19th century, the presence of a rabbi and two witnesses was sufficient. Some men are wearing a hat with a coloured brim, a *biritta*, specific to Italian Jews, and dark coats. The bridal dress was no different to fashionable Venetian clothing of the day; and a prayer shawl (*Tallit*) held above the bridal party's heads serves as a canopy (*Huppah*). The Jewish interior is recognisable from the two typical lamps hanging from the ceiling, and the seven-branched candelabrum. The two armchairs occupied by the notables are ceremonial chairs used for weddings and circumcisions. The second painting depicts a circumcision ceremony in a room with the windows wide open. Of the two circumcision chairs, often found in Jewish religious furniture in Italy, only one is occupied. The other, on a raised platform, has been left symbolically empty to welcome the spirit of the prophet Eliyah. Unusually, the newborn baby is being held by two men perched on a table, and the godfathers (*Sanddakim*) are both wearing *Tallit*. The chairs are similar to other Italian ceremonial chairs, like the one shown opposite.

Skull cap
Italy, 18th century
Satin, gold embroidery
20 x 29 cm
Strauss Collection,
Rothschild donation
On long-term loan
from the Musée national
du Moyen Âge, Paris
D.98.4.112

Bar Mitzvah

The *Bar Mitzvah* celebrates the religious coming of age of a boy on his thirteenth birthday. He is now considered responsible for fulfilling all the commandments and may become an active member of the Jewish community.

On the Monday or the Thursday preceding the *Shabbat*, wearing a prayer shawl (*Tallit*) with blue or black stripes and fringes (*Tzitzit*) hanging from the four corners, the boy puts on the *Tefillin* for the first time. These consist of little boxes containing tiny parchments on which the passages from the Bible setting out the main principles of Judaism are written. He binds them around his left arm and his head with leather straps.

The following *Shabbat*, after putting on the *Tefillin*, the *Bar Mitzvah* boy is called up for his first reading of the Torah. He reads all or a part of the portion (*Parashah*) for the week. He makes a speech (*Drashah*) displaying his religious knowledge. The ceremony is followed by a festive meal. During the nineteenth century, developments in Judaism led to the introduction of a *Bat Mitzvah* for twelve-year-old girls.

Small prayer shawl
(Tallit Katan)
Italy, 18th century
Satin, gold embroidery
41 x 35 cm
Strauss Collection,
Rothschild donation
On long-term loan
from the Musée national
du Moyen Âge, Paris
D.98.4.111

Marriage ring
Italy, 16th century
Gold and enamel
Diam.: 1.9 cm
Strauss Collection,
Rothschild donation
On long-term loan
from the Musée national
du Moyen Âge, Paris
D.98.4.36

Given by the bridegroom to his bride, the ring perpetuated the principle of acquisition practised in earliest Antiquity. The traditional Ashkenazi inscription *Mazal Tov* (good luck!), identifies this ring as Jewish; it expresses the wish that the event benefit from an auspicious configuration of the stars. The marriage ring was a family heirloom handed down from one generation to the next.

Marriage

In the Bible, conjugal love is seen as the epitome of holy perfection and is a metaphor for the union between God and His people, between Israel and the Torah. According to the Talmud, marriage is the ultimate purpose of divine creation.

In its rabbinical form, the ceremony begins with the betrothal, known as *Erusin* or *Kiddushin*, where the bridegroom weds his bride before two witnesses and in the presence of ten men. As he places the ring on her finger, thus sealing the *Kiddushin*, he declares: "Behold you are consecrated to me with this ring according to the law of Moses and Israel."; then the marriage contract, or *Ketubbah*, is read. It is signed by the husband and the witnesses before the marriage ceremony proper (*Nissu'in*) begins. The seven blessings or *Shev'a Berakhot* are recited under the *Huppah*, the canopy that symbolises the home that the couple are about to build. The wedding concludes with the newly-weds being left alone for some time.

Marriage contract,
Ketubbah
Modena, 1752
Parchment
88 x 61 cm
Strauss Collection,
Rothschild donation
On long-term loan
from the Musée national
du Moyen Âge, Paris
D.98.4.56

This is the marriage contract between Nathan, son of Eliyah Molho, and Gracia, daughter of Israel ha-Levi Orso, in the presence of witnesses, Menasseh Joshua, son of Rabbi Judah Masliah Padova and Abraham Hai, son of Rabbi Nethanael Gracia. At the bottom of the page are the stamps and signatures of the public translator, Moses of Rafael Vita Naso. In the central area, the text of the *Ketubbah* is written in square letters, next to that of the Conditions (*Tenaim*), in round letters of the Sephardi type. Verses 11 and 12 of Chapter 4 of the Book of Ruth form a frame on three sides. In the medallions, the four seasons and illustrations of Psalm 128 punctuate the frieze depicting the twelve signs of the Zodiac.

Ketubbah

The *Ketubbah* is a marriage contract required by Jewish law. Written in Aramaic, it sets out the obligations (*Tenaim*) of the husband towards his wife in their life together and in the event of divorce, in particular his financial responsibilities. The text records the date of the marriage, the place, the river running through the town, the bride's first name then that of the husband, followed by those of their respective fathers. It is preceded by the traditional formula: "Under a good sign! Under a good star!"

The first *Ketubbah*, dating back to the fifth century, was discovered in the *Genizah* at Cairo. From the Middle Ages, the art of illuminating marriage contracts developed, resulting, especially in Italy, in masterpieces of calligraphy and ornamentation.

The cycle of the year

Year 1 of the Jewish calendar, the year of the Creation, corresponds to the year 3761 BCE.

Because it is calculated according to the lunar cycle, the Jewish year does not correspond to the solar year. To compensate for this difference, a system was established with alternating years of twelve months (Nissan, Iyar, Sivvan, Tammuz, Av, Ellul, Tishri, Heshvan, Kislev, Tevet, Shevat and Adar), and leap years consisting of a thirteenth month, Adar II.

A day is counted from sunset to sunset. The cycle of the seasons is of primordial importance in the organisation of the calendar, and the festivals are bound up with the seasons and the months. The pilgrim festivals (*Shalosh Regalim*) have a dual significance: they are associated with the land because of their position in the agricultural year, and they commemorate milestones in the history of the Jewish people. In the month of Nissan, *Pesah*, takes place in the Spring, and commemorates the Exodus from Egypt; *Shavu'ot* celebrates the giving of the Torah to Moses as well as the harvest; *Sukkot* evokes the forty years spent wandering in the desert and celebrates the gathering of the crops.

The Jewish calendar

Month	*Dates*	*Festivals*
Nissan	15	First day of *Pesah*
Iyar	5	*Yom Ha'atzmaut* – Israel's Day of Independence
	18	*Lag ba-'Omer*
Sivan	6	*Shavu'ot*
Tammuz	17	Fast of Tammuz
Av	9	*Tisha b'Av* fast day
Elul		
Tishri	1 and 2	*Rosh ha-Shanah*
	10	*Yom Kippur*
	15	First day of *Sukkot*
	22	*Shemini 'Atzeret*
Heshvan		
Kislev	25	First day of *Hanukkah*
Tevet	10	Fast of Tevet
Shvat	15	*Tu Bi-Shevat*, New Year for Trees
Adar	14	*Purim*
Adar II	In a leap year, *Purim* is celebrated on 14 Adar II	

Scroll of Esther, *Megillah*
Salom Italia (attributed to)
Amsterdam, c. 1641
Carved wood, copperplate engraving on vellum
H. 48 (stave); 26.5 (parchment); L. 440 (8 pages, sewn together)
Gift of the Nahmias family
MAHJ 97.3.11

Salom Italia was born in Lisbon around 1619 and emigrated to Italy; he trained as an artist in Mantua and in the Venice region, and finally settled in Amsterdam in 1641. He is known for a portrait of the illustrious Menasseh Ben Israel but he was particularly famed for his *Megillah* illustrations, featuring characteristic arches with imposing pediments often supporting female figures: between the columns on this scroll the characters of the story are depicted: King Ahasuerus, Queen Esther, Haman and Mordekhai. The allegorical female figure on top of the arch represents victory and abundance. She is flanked alternately by helmeted angels and archangels. Salom Italia was in the habit of signing the frontispiece of his works. In this copy, the frontispiece was redone to add the owner's coat of arms. However, it is still possible to attribute this scroll to him, or at least recognize his strong influence.

Purim

***Purim*, the festival of lots, is celebrated on 14 Adar to commemorate the delivery of a plot to exterminate the Persian Jews. The account of this episode set in ancient Susa is recorded in the biblical Book of Esther. Haman, Vizier of King Ahasuerus (identified with the Persian King Xerxes II), had decided to kill all the Jews on 13 Adar, a date he chose by casting lots. In response to the appeal of her uncle Mordekhai, a descendant of King Saul, Queen Esther appealed to her husband, Ahasuerus, in order to thwart the plot. Haman and his sons were hanged.**

The rabbis made 13 Adar a day of fasting, followed on 14 by celebrations. On the evening before and the morning of the holiday, the Book of Esther is read in the synagogue. Every time the name of Haman is mentioned, the congregation drowns it out with the noise of rattles. The holiday ends with a large meal where the guests are encouraged to drink wine until they are unable to distinguish the names of Haman and Mordechai. It is customary to give food and pastries to friends, and gifts to the poor. Children wear fancy dress and plays are performed.

The *Megillah* or the Scroll of Esther

The illuminated *Megillot* made for private use appeared from the sixteenth century; until then, decorated scrolls were unknown. The scroll is written on parchment or paper, and is generally rolled around a single wooden stave. Later, the custom of making cases for the scrolls developed. Illuminators and etchers vied with each other to produce creative decorations between the columns or in strips at the bottom of the scroll, depicting scenes from the story and the main characters. Some artists made a name for themselves in this field, such as Arieh Leib from Góra (Poland), Salom Italia and Francesco Griselini.

4 The festival of Hanukkah

The festival of *Hanukkah* (dedication) is a post-biblical festival with no scriptural basis. Also called the Feast of Lights, it evokes a national reconstruction and a spiritual rebirth. *Hanukkah* commemorates the historic victory of the Maccabees over the Hellenistic dynasty of the Seleucids, the kings of Syria and Palestine, in 165 BCE. Mattathias the Hasmonean and his sons led the revolt of the Jews against King Antiochus IV Epiphanes, who had desecrated the Temple in Jerusalem. After their victory, the Jews rebuilt an altar, a candelabrum, and several pieces of synagogue furniture, which were inaugurated with grand festivities.

The holiday instituted by the rabbis of the Talmud begins on 25 Kislev. According to tradition, when Judah the Hasmonean entered the Temple, he discovered that only one small jar of oil for the candelabrum had escaped defilement, but, miraculously, this oil continued to burn for eight days. In commemoration of this event, a special eight-branched *Hanukkah* lamp is lit at nightfall for eight days, beginning with one light on the first day and adding another light each successive day. The lamp is placed in front of a window so that everyone can see it. In Ashkenazi communities and in Israel, the *Maoz Tsur* (*Rock of Ages*) is sung. The song was written in Germany in the thirteenth century. The Sephardim read Psalm 30.

Since the Middle Ages, *Hanukkah* has become a very popular holiday with its own customs. Special games are played with a spinning top and cards. It is also a children's holiday, and in the West, children receive gifts or small sums of money.

Lighting the candles
From the *Sefer ha-Minhagim* (Book of Ceremonies)
Amsterdam, Phoebus Ha Levi
1662

Hanukkah lamps

There are many kinds of *Hanukkah* lamps: all have eight lights and generally a *Shammash* (servant), an additional light which is used to kindle the others. The ancient Roman type, a flat oil lamp with compartments, or a multi-spouted terracotta lamp, was replaced, in the Middle Ages, by little bronze lamps with a triangular back plate, that were suspended, with decorations inspired by Gothic architecture. This form spread throughout Europe and North Africa with all sorts of ornamentation: flowers, biblical scenes, mythological characters, architectural motifs. From the sixteenth century, four feet were added, then the *Hanukkah* lamp became a candelabrum, more suited to synagogue use, and for holding candles.

***Hanukkah* lamp**
Germany, 16th century
Cast bronze
12 x 26 cm
MAHJ 94.10.1

***Hanukkah* lamp**
Alsace-Lorraine,
late 19th – early 20th century
Tin cutout (baking moulds)
17 x 30 x 9 cm
Gift of Georges Aboucaya
in memory of
Colette Aboucaya-Spira
MAHJ 96.3.3

***Hanukkah* lamp**
Comtat Venaissin,
16th or 17th century
Cast bronze
15.5 x 17.5 cm
Gift of Georges Aboucaya
in memory of
Colette Aboucaya-Spira
MAHJ 91.12.1

***Hanukkah* lamp**
Italy, 16th century
Bronze
11 x 21 x 5.5 cm
Gift of René Wiener
On long-term loan
from the Musée historique
lorrain, Nancy
D.96.4.22

Hanukkah **lamp**
Breslau, Germany, 18th century
Partial-gilt silver,
embossed and engraved
37 x 37.5 x 5 cm
Hillet-Monoach bequest
On long-term loan
from the Musée national
du Moyen Âge, Paris
D. 98.4.24

Hanukkah **lamp**
Italy, 16th century
Bronze
16.5 x 21 x 6 cm
Strauss Collection,
Rothschild donation
On long-term loan
from the Musée national
du Moyen Âge, Paris
D.98.4.19

Hanukkah **lamp**
Morocco, 19th century
Engraved cast bronze
29.5 x 23.3 x 7.5 cm
Gift of the Musée d'Art juif
de Paris
MAHJ 2002.1.456

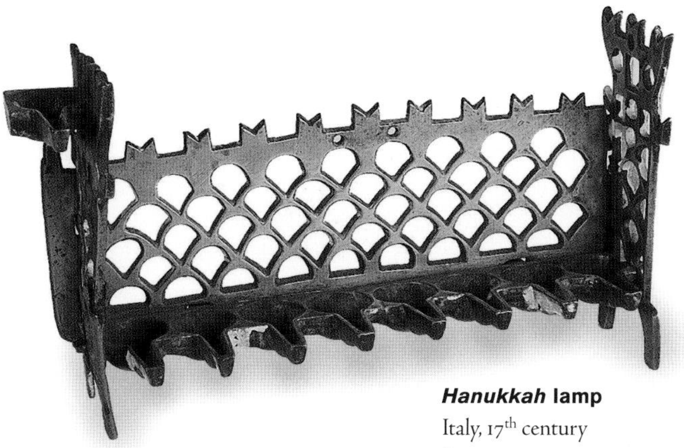

Hanukkah **lamp**
Italy, 17th century
Bronze
15 x 28 x 7 cm
Gift of René Wiener
On long-term loan
from the Musée historique
lorrain, Nancy
D.96.4.19

Hanukkah **lamp**
North Africa, 18th century
(based on a 16th century
Sicilian model)
Engraved cast bronze
16.6 x 20 x 6.8 cm
Gift of the Musée d'Art juif
de Paris
MAHJ 2002.1.692

Hanukkah **lamp**
Rabat, 19th or 20th century
Bronze
22.5 x 21.5 cm
Gift of Georges Aboucaya
in memory of
Colette Aboucaya-Spira
MAHJ 96.3.6

Sefer Tehillim
Robert Estienne, Paris, 1545
Red morocco, laid paper
10.5 x 6.5 cm
Gift of Georges Aboucaya
in memory of Colette
Aboucaya-Spira
MAHJ 91.12.124

This Book of Psalms, or *Sefer Tehillim*, was part of a small-format Bible in seventeen volumes, printed between 1544 and 1546, in Paris, by Robert Estienne, master printer to King François I for publications in Hebrew. This volume is a fine example of Hebrew printing during the Renaissance. In addition to the Psalms, it contains the Proverbs, Job, the five scrolls, or *Megillot*: and the Song of Songs, the Book of Ruth, Lamentations, Ecclesiastes and the Book of Esther. The title page bears Robert Estienne's imprint.

Hebrew printing

Between the fifteenth and the eighteenth centuries, Hebrew printing developed in Europe, thanks as much to Christian as to Jewish printers. France very nearly became the cradle of Hebrew typography, as evidenced by a contract dated 1443 and drawn up in Avignon, commissioning a set of Hebrew printing characters. But it was in 1474, in Reggio di Calabria, in Italy, that the first printed Hebrew book was published, Rashi's commentary on the Pentateuch.

Printing developed at an early stage in Spain and Portugal, but was short-lived, disrupted by the persecutions and brought to an end with the expulsion. The Portuguese refugees en route for the Ottoman Empire made a brief halt in Morocco, then in Italy. In 1484, Joshua Salomon Soncino published the treatise *Berakhot* of the Babylon Talmud, then in 1488, the first printed Hebrew Bible. On reaching Ottoman soil, the brothers Nahmias and Sasson established printing presses in Constantinople in 1493, and in Salonika in 1513.

The first *Haggadah* was printed in Prague, in 1526, but the most famous Prague printing works was that of the Bak family, established in 1605. In Germany, the first Jewish printers did not emerge until the beginning of the seventeenth century, publishing numerous translations and compilations in Judeo-German. In Poland, from 1534, Cracow and then Lublin became major printing centres.

In the early sixteenth century, around the major faculties of theology such as Basle and Paris, Christian printers published works in Hebrew. In Paris, the Estienne firm employed the engraver Guillaume le Bé and published two Bibles considered as masterpieces of Hebrew typography. In Antwerp, in 1549, Plantin published a Bible, and Hebrew grammar manuals and dictionaries. In Venice, from 1516 to 1549, Daniel Bomberg was the first to publish the Pentateuch (1517), and the two complete editions of the Talmud (from 1520 to 1523).

Amsterdam was responsible for the following typographical innovation: in 1626, Menasseh ben Israel created the *Otiyot Amsterdam* or "Amsterdam characters" which became the dominant typography in Europe. Two families, the Athias and the Proops made Amsterdam a leading Hebrew printing centre, vying with Venice, until the nineteenth century when Poland and Germany became the most innovative and dynamic centres.

H̲iddushei ha-Torah
(*novellae* or "new insights" into the Torah)
Moses ben Nah̲man
(known as Nah̲manides or RaMbaN, 1194-1270)
Lisbon, 1489
Gift of the Nahmias family
MAHJ 98.29.1

This commentary on the Pentateuch is the first book in any language to have been printed in Lisbon. It contains only Nah̲manides' commentary, without the Biblical text. It is printed in Rashi characters, in two columns. The work was edited by the scholar David ibn Yah̲ia and printed by Eliezer ben Jacob Toledano, who had set up the first printing press in his home. The same year, he published the *Perush ha-berakhot ve-ha-tefillot* by the Talmud scholar David Abudarham.

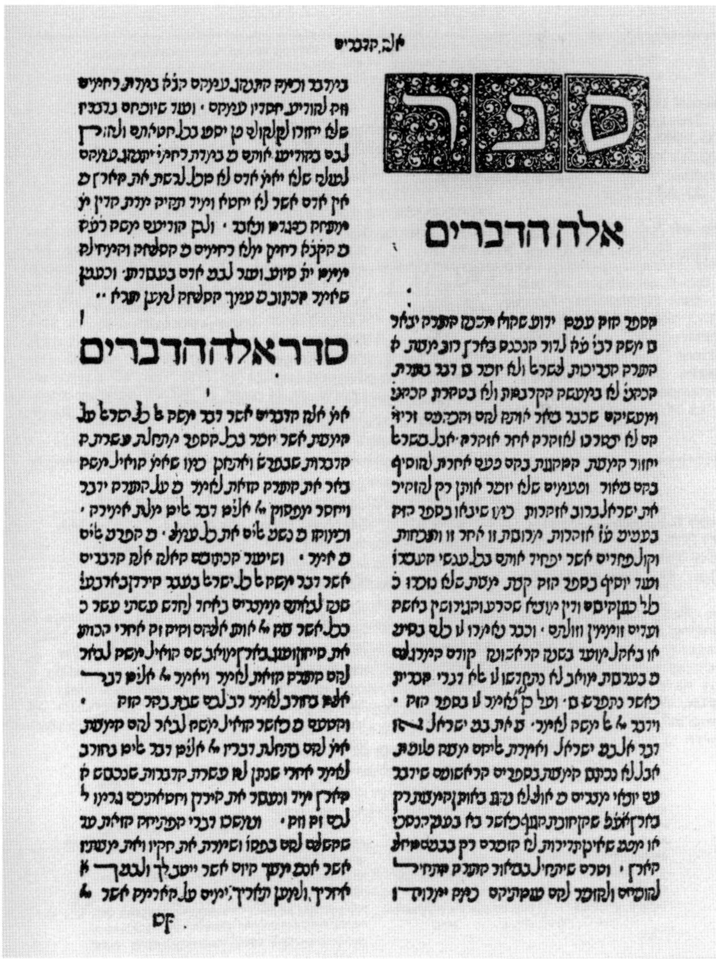
אלה הדברים

ספר

אלה הדברים

סדר אלה הדברים

5 Amsterdam, The meeting point of two diasporas

The Dedication of the Portuguese Synagogue in Amsterdam
Bernard Picart
(b. 1673, Paris - d. 1733 Amsterdam)
London, 1733
Etching on laid paper
31.7 x 41.5 cm
Gift of the Musée d'Art juif de Paris
MAHJ 2002.1.278

The Portuguese Synagogue built by Elias Bouman, was planned some forty years after the three Sephardi communities in Amsterdam joined forces to welcome a steadily growing number of worshippers. The foundation stone was laid by David van Isaac da Pinto, in 1671, and the Synagogue was inaugurated in August 1675. Although it resembles the Protestant churches of the 17th century in style, its layout is reminiscent of that of the Temple of Solomon, a model of which, created by Jacob Judah Leon "Templo", inspired the plans for the enlargement of the synagogue in the 18th century.

Between 1595 and 1600, converted Jews, originally from the Iberian peninsula, began to flock to Amsterdam. These Marranos, or new Christians, had secretly remained faithful to Judaism, and were fleeing the Inquisition in the hope of finding security in the United Provinces of the Netherlands, the first republic in Europe to recognise religious freedom. Amsterdam permitted the free revival of a religion that was despised throughout the rest of Europe at that time, for these "Portuguese" emerged from clandestine practice to revive the religion of their ancestors, after several generations. Often ignorant of the foundations of Judaism, they had to undergo a thorough religious apprenticeship. Some of them developed innovative points of view compared with rabbinical Judaism, which led to their being accused of heresy and being excommunicated by the rabbinical authorities. Such was the case of Uriel da Costa, whose work *Examen dos Tradiçoes Phariseas Conferidas con a Ley Escrita* was publicly burned in 1624, and of Baruch Spinoza, author of the famous *Tractatus Theologico-Politicus*, who left Amsterdam around 1660 and opted for the Latin translation of his first name, Benedictus.

Among the Portuguese Jews who had settled in Amsterdam were a number of merchants who contributed to the city's economic boom as it grew increasingly prosperous. Some of them were founders of the Dutch East India Company and developed commerce with the major European trading centres (Bayonne, Nantes, La Rochelle, Hamburg, London), and with the Mediterranean world and the colonies. In Amsterdam itself, they helped the economic sectors to which they had access to flourish, despite opposition from the guilds: the silk, sugar, tobacco and diamond industries.

In tandem with this financial prosperity, they developed an intense cultural life. The heart of the Hebrew printing industry, Amsterdam was nicknamed the "Jerusalem of Holland".

The intellectual activities of the Amsterdam Jews covered every conceivable area.

The ravages of the Thirty Years' War prompted Ashkenazi Jews from Central and Eastern Europe to settle in Amsterdam around 1635. The years 1655-1660 saw the arrival of Jews fleeing the massacres in Poland. Their material situation was much less favourable than that of their Sephardi predecessors, who were not particularly enthusiastic at the arrival of these destitute refugees, and were anxious to protect their own respectability.

The Jewish community was therefore indisputably riven with socio-cultural divisions, and it underwent several profound doctrinal crises, such as that of Shabbataianism. But beyond all these difficulties, Amsterdam permitted the revival of a religion which at the time was prohibited in the rest of Western Europe.

BENOIT SPINOSA
Né à Amsterdam, l'An 1632. Mort le
21. Février 1677. Agé de 44 ans.

Portrait of Spinoza
France, 17th century
Copperplate engraving
on laid paper
14.1 x 9.7 cm
Gift of the Musée d'Art juif
de Paris
MAHJ 2002.1.250

Born into a Marrano family that had settled in Amsterdam, the philosopher Benedictus (Baruch) Spinoza (b.1632, Amsterdam, d. 1677, The Hague) received a traditional Jewish education before studying Latin and Jewish and Christian philosophy. He read Descartes, and became a freethinker and critic, a supporter of rationalist modernity in religious thinking. This position incurred the wrath of the religious authorities, who considered him an atheist and a heretic. The Jewish community imposed the *Herem* (excommunication) on him in 1656, after which he was exiled in 1660. Many consider his *Tractatus Theologico-Politicus* (1670) and his main work, *Ethica* (published posthumously in 1677), as a negation of the fundamental principles of Judaism and a threat to the religion.

Torah finials, *Rimmonim*
The Hague, c. 1763
Silver, cast,
chased and parcel-gilt
44 x 12 cm
Private collection
D.97.4.1

These ornaments in the form of a tower are typical of the *Rimmonim* made in Holland, inspired by church bell towers. They were dedicated to the Synagogue by Samuel de Pinto, who belonged to one of the most illustrious Portuguese Marrano families in the Netherlands. The Pinto brothers had settled in Rotterdam in 1646, and there they established a trade bank and set up a *Yeshivah* which they transferred to Amsterdam, where they settled in 1669. They soon became the most powerful family in the Portuguese community, and founded a new synagogue, the famous *Esnoga*. The family had extensive ramifications; Samuel de Pinto was less well known than his contemporary Isaac de Pinto, the philosopher who challenged Voltaire on the subject of his opinions on the Jews.

Bernard Picart (b. 1673, Paris, d. 1733, Amsterdam)
"Manière de conduire les Époux de la Loi"
(Procession of the Bridegrooms of the Law)
Amsterdam, 1723
Etching, 15.1 x 21.1 cm
MAHJ 94.24.1

This extraordinarily detailed etching depicts the procession during the festival of *Simhat Torah* when the Jewish community honours those who have been chosen, one to bless the reading of the last portion of the Torah, and the other to bless the beginning of the new annual cycle of the reading of the Pentateuch.

Bernard Picart (b. 1673, Paris, d. 1733, Amsterdam)
"L'examen du levain"
(Searching for leaven)
Amsterdam, 1725
Etching, 14.9 x 20.4 cm
MAHJ 96.08.1

"For seven days you shall eat unleavened cakes. On the very first day you shall rid your houses of leaven" (Exodus 12:15). The search for leaven, *Bedikat hametz*, is carried out by the master of the house in the night preceding *Pesah* (from 13 to 14 Nissan). This family ritual takes place at nightfall, by candlelight.

Bernard Picart (b. 1673, Paris - d. 1733, Amsterdam)

Bernard Picart, a French Protestant who found refuge in Amsterdam in 1710 was the author of the book entitled *Cérémonies et coutumes religieuses de tous les peuples du monde* (Religious ceremonies and customs of all the peoples of the world). The section of the book devoted to Jewish rituals is a unique testimony to the life of the Portuguese and Ashkenazi Jewish communities of Amsterdam at the beginning of the eighteenth century. The engravings depict with great accuracy the ceremonies that make up Jewish life: circumcision, marriage, funeral rites, and the festivals that take place within the home, preparations for the Passover meal, the feast of Tabernacles and meals under the *Sukkah*, as well as religious services in the synagogue.

The Jews of Amsterdam inspired numerous artists, but Picart was able to identify the social differences and divergent practices of the two communities. His portrayal, while not omitting any of the most striking customs for an outsider, remains faithful and sympathetic. Apart from reprints of the book in the years after its publication, the success of this particular series of engravings devoted to the religion gave rise to countless imitations in the eighteenth century, in England (Philips) and in Italy (Novelli).

DIT IS DE POORT DES EEU
WIGEN, DE REGTVAARDI
GEN TREDEN DAAR DOOR
BINNEN, MET VREDE!!!
TSEBAOT
DAT IN DEN HEMEL VOOR ONS
VERDIENSTEN MOGEN ZIJN
ZOEK
DEN
VRE
DE
ONZE GOD
MIJN ROTS
GELOOFD ZIJ DE MAJES-
TEIT DES EEUWIGEN!!!
JAAR!
HEIL
ONS

6 "Next year in Jerusalem"

Decorative panel for the eastern wall of a room, *Mizrah*
Levi David van Gelder
Netherlands, 1843
Ink drawing
74 x 60.5 cm
Gift of Georges Aboucaya in memory of Colette Aboucaya-Spira
MAHJ 91.12.35

This extraordinary drawing draws on a hugely varied range of iconographic sources; it belongs to the Jewish tradition of micrography, a technique that consists of using lines of text to make up the lines of the drawing. The architectural structure of the composition is in keeping with a frequent desire to evoke the Temple of Jerusalem in this type of picture. The iconography mixes Biblical characters, Moses and Aaron, the Prophet Elijah and King David. The artist has created a parallel between the Temple instruments and furniture and masonic symbols. Levi van Gelder, who was known for other works in the same genre, emigrated to the United States in 1860.

Around the year 1000 BCE, King David, anxious to ensure the unity of the twelve tribes of Israel, established his capital in a little independent city in the hills of Judaea, and immediately installed the Holy Ark in which the Tablets of the Law were kept. His successor, King Solomon, built a temple there. Destroyed for the first time by the Babylonians in 585 BCE, Jerusalem was rebuilt by Ezra and Nehemiah. Later, King Herod (40-3 BCE) rebuilt his temple to make it one of the splendours of Antiquity. Jerusalem became a major centre for sacrifices and pilgrimages, a place where people argued about God and his Law. But it was destroyed a second time by the Romans in the year 70 CE, and the city's defenders were dispersed to all four corners of the earth. From then on, the exiles never stopped cherishing the dream of restoring the city, nurturing in their collective and individual memories the image of a celestial Jerusalem and hoping for its fulfilment in the earthly Jerusalem.

In their homes, Jews mark the direction of Jerusalem and turn towards it when they pray. In their prayers, they ask for Jerusalem to be rebuilt, tirelessly repeating the famous verse from Psalms "If I forget you, O Jerusalem, let my right hand wither away" (137:5). They keep no less than three fast days a year as a symbol of mourning and do not conclude the Passover ceremony or the Yom Kippur service without saying: "Next year in Jerusalem".

Pilgrimage

The Bible (Deuteronomy 16:16) recommends that all adult Jewish males should make a pilgrimage three times a year to appear before God in His holy place: on *Pesah* (Passover), *Shavu'ot* (the Festival of Weeks, Pentecost), and *Sukkot*, (the Festival of Booths or Tabernacles) and make sacrifices and offerings. These festivals are particularly important and are associated with the commemoration of key moments in the history of the Jews and of the agricultural year.

Pesah begins on 15 Nissan (in March-April) and lasts for seven days. The festival celebrates the deliverance of the children of Israel from Egyptian bondage. On the eve of their departure, they sacrificed a lamb which they ate with bitter herbs. They daubed its blood on the lintel and doorposts of their homes to secure divine protection so that death would pass over their households, claiming only the eldest sons of the Egyptians. Then, led by Moses, they departed in haste, taking dough that had not had time to rise.

Throughout the festival, only *Matzah* and food that does not contain leaven are eaten. On the first night, all the members of the family come together for the *Seder*, a ceremony following a prescribed order that retells the story of the Exodus from Egypt (*Haggadah*). The *Pesah* liturgical tradition includes the formula "next year in Jerusalem" and the reading of the *Song of Songs*, which contains an allusion to spring, for *Pesah* is also the festival of the return of spring.

Shavu'ot takes place seven weeks after *Pesah*, on 6 and 7 Sivan (May-June). It is both the harvest festival and that of the first fruits (*Bikkurim*), which the ancient Israelites took to the Temple as offerings, as well as the celebration of the giving of the Law to Moses on Mount Sinai.

On this occasion, the synagogues and homes are decorated with flowers and plants, and dairy and fruit-based foods are eaten. Then, in many traditional communities, the night is devoted to study. For *Shavu'ot* it is customary to read the complete story of Ruth, the symbol of fidelity to the Jewish faith.

***Pesah* prayer book**
Haggadah Beit Horin
Dorvasy, engraver
after Jacob Proops,
Moses May, printer
Metz and Nancy, 1767
22.5 x 17.5 cm
Anonymous gift
MAHJ 92.5.2

This Passover *Haggadah* entitled *Beit Horin* (House of Free Men), is written in Hebrew and Judeo-German. The copperplate engravings are inspired by the illustrations in the *Haggadah* published by Jacob Proops in Amsterdam. Moses May of Metz was the first Jewish printer to be granted royal authorisation to print books in Hebrew and Judeo-German.

***Seder* dish**
Nuremberg?, 1773
Engraved pewter
Diam. 31.5 cm
Gift of René Wiener
On long-term loan
from the Musée historique
lorrain, Nancy
D.96.4.29

This dish is typical of those found in the German area and in Central Europe. The inscriptions are related to the festival: order of the ceremony and ritual elements, while the letters in the centre give the date as 1773. The figures of Adam and Eve, surprising in this context, suggest that it could have been a wedding present. It is not unusual to find the blazons or emblems of the ruling monarch on Jewish ritual objects. Here, for example, we find the crowned two-headed eagle. Often signs of allegiance, they are imbued with allusions.

The *Seder*

The *Seder*, which begins the festival of *Pesah*, is entirely symbolic, and should prompt each participant to consider themselves as having been freed from Egypt. In front of the master of the house a dish is placed on which various items of food have been arranged, each with a special significance: a shankbone, which represents the paschal lamb; an egg, traditionally eaten by those in mourning and here recalling the destruction of the Temple in Jerusalem; bitter herbs, evoking slavery; *haroset*, a mixture of fruits, spices and red wine representing the mortar the children of Israel made to build the pyramids; green leaves; and salt water into which some of these ingredients are dipped.

Booth for the feast of Tabernacles, *Sukkah*
Austria or South Germany
late 19th century
Painted pine
220 x 285.5 cm
Acquired with the help of the Fonds du Patrimoine (heritage fund) and the generosity of Claire Maratier
MAHJ 89.1.1

"You shall live in booths for seven days, all who are native Israelites ..." (Leviticus 23:42). A makeshift construction with a roof of branches, this *Sukkah* or booth is used for the entire duration of the festival of *Sukkot*. The décor is traditional and at the same time shows a perfect assimilation of local crafts. Its walls are decorated with picturesque views of an Austrian village, a shield inscribed with the first few words of the Decalogue and a floral decoration evoking the agricultural significance of the festival. The main panel depicts Jerusalem, in a style common from the second half of the 19th century, showing the walls, the hills, the Dome of the Rock, the El Aqsa Mosque and, in the centre, the Wailing Wall.

Sukkot, begins on the 15th of Tishri (September-October) and ends on the eighth day with *Simẖat Torah* (the Rejoicing of the Torah). During this festival of harvest and plenty, meals should be taken in a *Sukkah*, a booth with a roof of branches whose sparse protection is intended to evoke the precariousness of human existence during the forty years in the wilderness. Each morning of the festival, the full *Hallel* is recited , and, on the eighth day, the prayer for rain in the Holy Land. The congregation shakes the *Lulav*, consisting of four species of plant: a palm branch, a myrtle twig, a willow bough and a citron, symbols of the solidarity between the diverse groups that make up the Jewish people.

Jewish messianism

The fall of the Kingdom of Judaea, in 587-586 BCE, and the captivity in Babylon made the Jews hope for a Messiah who would liberate them and lead his people back to the Holy Land. The various foreign occupations, until the destruction of the Temple by the Roman army under Titus in the year 70 CE, heightened this expectation even further. The messianic idea appealed to many Jews, but also to Christians, and, during the course of history, false messiahs emerged, such as David Reuveni in the sixteenth century, Shabbetai Tsevi in the seventeenth century, and then Jacob Frank.

Le Vray Portraict de SABETHA SEBI
Roy des Juifs né en la ville de ſmirne en
Asie aagé de 40. Ans

"Le Vray Portraict de Sabetha Sebi, Roy de Juifs"
(The true portrait of Shabtai Zvi, King of the Jews)
after Johannes and Cornelis Meyssens
Netherlands, late 17th century
Engraving
22.9 x 16.2 cm
MAHJ 95.27.1

A rabbi at the age of 18, Shabbetai Tsevi (b. 1626, Smyrna d. 1676, Albania) rapidly crossed the threshold between mystical asceticism and Messianic exaltation. From 1648, deeply dismayed by the massacres perpetrated by the Cossacks of Chmielnicki, he developed messianic pretensions which found support among the troubled Jewish communities throughout Europe. Expelled from Smyrna in 1651, he led an errant existence in the Mediterranean countries. His proclamations however threatened the authority of the Sultan, who had him imprisoned and forced him to convert to Islam (1666), then banished him. His conversion felt like a betrayal to the many faithful, but it did not completely destroy the Shabbateian movement, a powerful, lasting tremor whose repercussions continued to be felt until the end of the 18th century.

7 The traditional Ashkenazi world

In the eleventh century, the Hebrew word *Ashkenaz* was used to designate the north of former Lotharingia, a region encompassing part of the former Carolingian empire: north-eastern France, Lorraine, Flanders and the Rhineland. Until the end of the twelfth century, the Ashkenazi Jewish communities lived in an area including France, England, the Netherlands, Germany west of the Elbe, Switzerland and northern Italy.

Successive waves of persecutions and expulsions between the thirteenth and the seventeenth centuries caused these communities to emigrate towards Eastern Europe, pushing out the geographical boundaries of Ashkenazi Judaism. The Jews of England and France fled to Germany, Austria, Poland and Russia, extending the Ashkenazi area from the North Sea to Italy, and from Alsace to Kiev. The end of the nineteenth century saw violent pogroms in the Russian Empire, which caused large numbers of Jews to emigrate to Western Europe and the American continent. Mainly in the eastern part, this area was defined by *Yiddishkeit*, a culture based on a way of life and a language, Yiddish, which appeared around the tenth century and was the chief means of communication of eleven million Jews just prior to World War II. At this time, most of the world's Jews belonged to Ashkenazi communities.

Although the fundaments of the faith are the same, there are differences between the liturgy of the Sephardim (Jews of Spanish origin) and that of the Ashkenazim. The Rhineland communities and, more broadly, those of north-eastern Europe, refer to the Jerusalem Talmud, whereas the Sephardi Jews are influenced by that of Babylon. Mediaeval Rhineland Judaism, practised in Central and Eastern Europe, is the basis of Ashkenazi synagogue worship, with a few regional variations. It is characterised by fidelity to the *Halakhah* (the body of Jewish law) and by its rigour, as well as

Synagogue of Jezyory, Lithuania
Early 20th century,
black and white photograph
Gift of the Musée d'Art Juif de Paris
MAHJ ph/113.16

by the importance accorded to religious study. In the mid-sixteenth century, Rabbi Moses Ben Isserles, author of *Ha-Mappah* (*The Tablecloth*), added to the strict religious code developed a few years earlier by Joseph Caro in the *Shul'han 'Arukh* (*The Well-Laid Table*) and included questions of custom (*minhag*) specific to the Ashkenazi world.

However this world did not remain rigid, and was soon caught up in religious controversies and conflicts of ideas similar to the clashes of the eighteenth century between the advocates of Hasidism, a popular mystical movement founded by the Baal Shem Tov, and their opponents, the *Mitnagdim* of the Vilna Gaon. It was also from these communities that the main modern religious trends developed – Reform Judaism, Neo-orthodoxy and Conservative Judaism. Furthermore, the first theorists and pioneers of Zionism mainly came from the Ashkenazi world, while others opted rather to participate in the revolutionary struggle, particularly within the Bund, founded in 1897. The model of traditional Jewish communities thus gave way to a number of different expressions of identity.

תקון קריאת שמע

השכיבנו ײ אלהינו לשלום ו

והעמידנו מלכנו ל

לחיים ופרוס עלינו סכת שלומך ותקננו

בעצה טובה מלפניך והושיענו למען שמך

והגן בעדנו והסר מעלינו אויב דבר וחרב

ורעב ויגון · והסר שטן מלפנינו ומאחרינו

ובצל כנפיך תסתירני · כי ײ שומרנו ו

ומצילנו אתה · כי ײ מלך חנון ורחום

אתה · ושמור צאתנו ובואנו לחיים ו

ולשלום מעתה ועד עולם :

Prayer book, *Mahzor*
Levi Offenbach, scribe
Nancy, 1767
Ink on parchment, full leather binding, gold lettering
10.6 x 7.5 cm
Gift of Théo Klein
MAHJ 96.52.1

Model of the synagogue in Wolpa, Byelorussia
Made by students at the ORT schools in Paris, 20th century
Wood
41.5 x 42 x 28.5 cm
Gift of the Musée d'Art juif de Paris
MAHJ 2002.1.414

The originality of the architectural design of the wooden synagogue in Wolpa, dating back to 1643, inspired many later synagogue buildings. Its interior design was unique, with an extraordinary interplay of vaults and galleries.
The dominant feature was a monumental *Bimah*, surrounded by four pillars more than 14 metres high, which supported the ceiling dome. The decorative motifs of the ten-metre-high *Aron ha-Kodesh*, are taken from traditional Jewish iconography and incorporate symbols associated with the Temple in Jerusalem, the Yachin and Boaz columns, the *menorah*.
The synagogue was burned down by the Nazis during World War II.

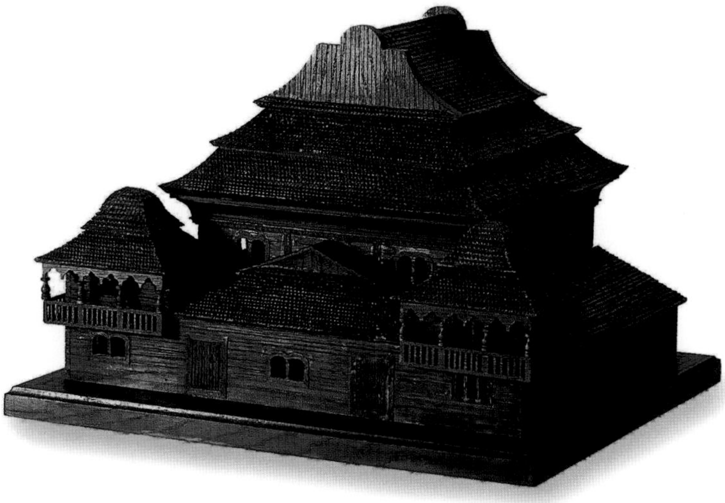

Synagogue architecture

The synagogues built in Poland, Ukraine and Lithuania in the latter half of the sixteenth century and during the seventeenth century, are among the most remarkable examples of traditional synagogue architecture. Inspired by local wooden buildings, churches in particular, they were particularly distinctive for their pagoda-style two or three-tiered roofs with three or four sides. In contrast with the austere exterior of the building, the elegant interior was lavishly decorated with multi-coloured frescos, inscriptions and carved wooden furniture.

The synagogues in towns, usually built outside the walls, were more imposing masonry edifices, like fortresses, and were much less remarkable to look at. These buildings provided a safe refuge during pogroms and wars.

Very few wooden synagogues remain today; some fortress synagogues, including the Old Synagogue in Cracow, have survived unscathed.

Model of the synagogue in Zolkiew, Galicia, Lvov region (Lemberg)
Made by students at the schools of the ORT in Paris, 1949
Plaster
64 x 60 x 40 cm
Gift of the Musée d'Art juif de Paris
MAHJ 2002.1.408

From the sixteenth century Zolkiew was home to a large Jewish community.
The Chmielnicki massacres in 1648 prompted the Jews to seek the right to build a fortress synagogue, which John III Sobieski granted them in 1687. The square form of this imposing building was supported by pillars, between which was the *Bimah*, surrounded by an ornamental structure in wrought iron. Leaning against the eastern wall was a carved wooden *Aron ha-Kodesh* on three levels.
The synagogue was destroyed by the Nazis in 1941.

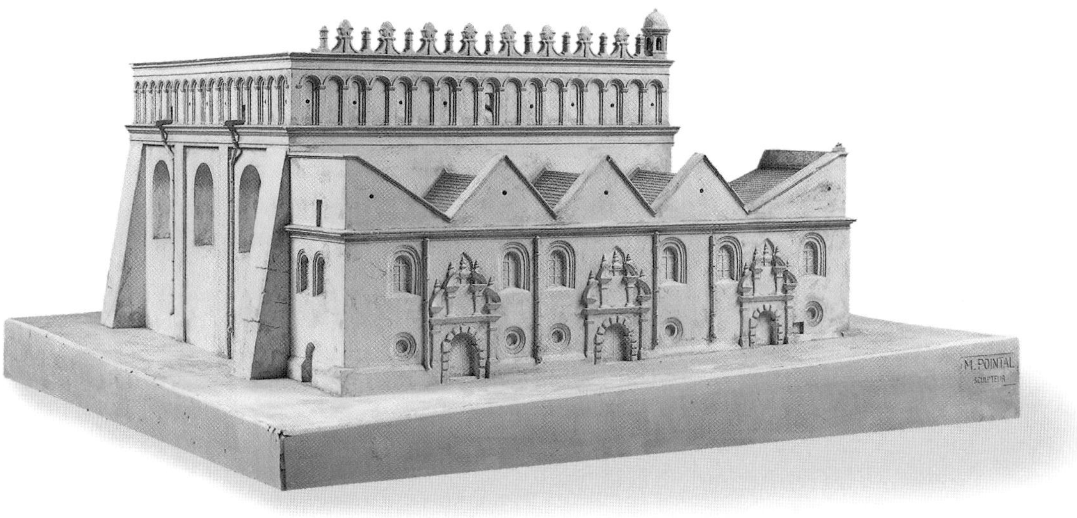

Samuel Hirszenberg
(b. 1865, Lodz,
d. 1908, Jerusalem)
The Jewish Cemetery
Munich ?, 1892
Oil on canvas
200 x 297 cm
Acquired courtesy
of Claude Kelman
MAHJ 92.1.1

This painting, acclaimed during the artist's lifetime as a masterpiece, typifies the devastation of the Jewish communities as a result of the pogroms that began in the 1880s in Poland and Russia. The despairing attitudes of the three weeping women among the tombstones, expresses the anguish of the Jews confronting a crucial phase of their history. The composition, dominated by dark colours and strong contrasts, is inspired by the memory of the cemetery in Cracow. This painting shows the influence of Corot and Courbet on the artist, who stayed in Paris, and of the Russian movement of the Itinerants, painters who broke with the official trends to depict social reality.

Mezuzah case
Germany, 17th-18th century
Carved wood
16 x 3.5 x 2.2 cm
Strauss Collection,
Rothschild donation
On long-term loan
from the Musée national
du Moyen Âge, Paris
D.98.4.64

The *Mezuzah* is a little scroll of parchment on which two passages from Deuteronomy are written – 4:4-9 and 9:13-21. This scroll is placed in a case which is attached to the doorpost in accordance with the command: "write them [God's words] on the doorposts of your houses and on your gates." (Deuteronomy, 6:9). The *Mezuzah* is a reminder of the sanctity of the home and places it under divine protection. The case has an architectural form, with an arched window reminiscent of late Romanesque style. It is crowned by two eagle heads facing opposite directions. The window allows the word *Shaddai* to be seen – this is an acronym of *Shomer dlatot Yisrael,* guardian of the gates of Israel, which is written on the back of the *Mezuzah*.

Ark and Torah scroll
Caspar Zacharias Raiman
Vienna, 1700-1709
Silver, repoussé, engraved, parcel-gilt and glass beads
56 x 21 x 14.5 cm
Strauss Collection, Rothschild donation
On long-term loan from the Musée national du Moyen Âge, Paris
D.98.4.125

This type of Ark was made for the Jews who had a private prayer room in their home or wanted to take a Torah with them on their travels. This highly ornate Ark is unique. The Torah scrolls, mantle and binder have been preserved. The inscription on the binder links it to Samson Wertheimer (b. 1658, Worms, d. 1724, Vienna), and bears he name of his grandson, Joseph ben Simon Wolf Wertheimer. Related to the Oppenheimer family, Samson Wertheimer, a court Jew in Vienna, was entrusted with the administration of the property of three emperors between 1694 and 1709: Leopold I, Joseph I and Charles VI. A great financier and community leader, he intervened on behalf of the threatened Jewish communities in Worms, Frankfurt and Rothenburg, and of those in war-torn Hungary, which earned him the title of Chief Rabbi. A philanthropist and scholar, he built synagogues and funded Talmudic schools and the printing of the Talmud in Frankfurt (1712-1722).

Torah crown
Workshop of Aryeh Leib Katz (?)
Lemberg, (Austria-Hungary),
late 18th century
Silver, silver gilt, enamel
and semiprecious stones
39 x 16.8 cm
Hallmarks: Lemberg, 1809-1810
On long-term loan
from the Consistory of Paris
D.95.3.1

While the Jews of western Europe were excluded from the craft corporations and guilds, in the regions of the Austro-Hungarian Empire, Galicia and the Ukraine, they were allowed to work as goldsmiths within specific corporations. This closed crown with six curved vertical elements supports a smaller crown topped by a sphere on which an eagle is perched. The positioning of the crowns one above the other illustrates a rabbinic quotation: "There are three crowns: the crown of the Torah, the crown of the priesthood and the crown of royalty; but the crown of a good reputation surpasses them all." (Mishnah, *Lessons of the Fathers of the World*, 4:13). The decoration consists of six quadrilobed enamelled medallions, two decorated with bouquets of flowers, and the other four with Hebrew inscriptions referring to Jacob's dream, Aaron, Moses and the Ark of the Covenant. The name of the donor can be seen on one of them, Abraham, son of Mekhel. The goldsmith Aryeh Leib Katz and his successors produced several similar crowns.

Ark curtain, *Parokhet*
France, 1791
Brocade silk
195 x 109 cm
On long-term loan from
the Musée historique lorrain,
Nancy
D.96.4.36.1

Ornamental Torah shield, *Tas*
Germany, early 18th century
Pierced and gilded cast silver
18 x 24.8 cm
Strauss Collection,
Rothschild donation
On long-term loan
from the Musée national
du Moyen Âge, Paris
D.98.4.145

The decoration of this shield with its traditional motifs evokes the Torah and the Temple: crown, lions, fleurs de lys and pillars. This symbolism is reinforced by two cherubs reminiscent of the *Kerubbim* guarding the divine throne, and two angels, both placed beneath a crown. In the central sliding compartment is a plate engraved with the festival being celebrated.

Torah finials, *Rimmonim*
Austria-Hungary, 18th century
Silver, chased, repoussé,
parcel-gilt and cast
44 x 13.5 cm
On long-term loan from
the Consistory of Paris
D.96.2.5.1-2

Pointer, *Yad*
Galicia, c. 1800
Silver, parcel-gilt
H. 21 cm
Strauss Collection,
Rothschild donation
On long-term loan
from the Musée national
du Moyen Âge, Paris
D.98.4.155

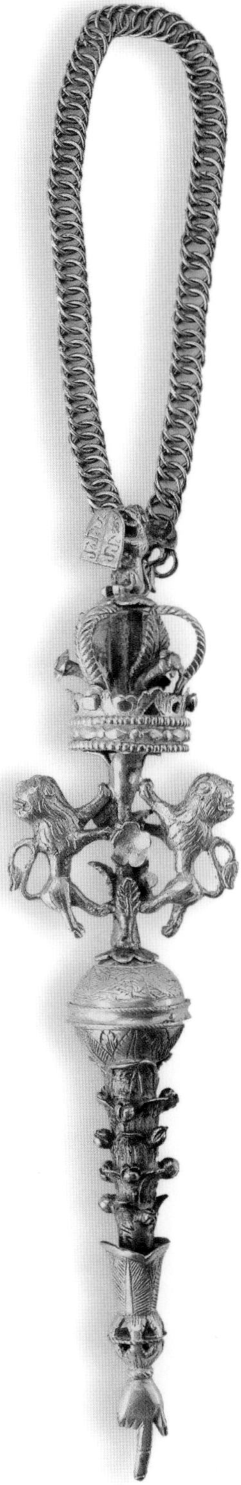

The Sabbath

"God blessed the seventh day and made it holy, because on that day he ceased from all the work he had set himself to do." (Genesis 2:3). The Sixth Commandment adds a social dimension to the holy nature of the Sabbath for it requires the entire family to rest, including the servants and the animals (Exodus 20: 8–11). This day of respite at the end of the week is celebrated by ceasing all activities that would change the order of things –natural, mechanical or social.

The respite from daily toil is accompanied by a number of ritual and spiritual acts that highlight the special nature of this day. Hailed as a queen, *Shabbat ha-Malkah*, the Sabbath is welcomed in on Friday evening, before nightfall, with psalms, *Kabbalat Shabbat*, followed by *Kiddush*, the sanctification of the day, recited over a cup of wine. Two candles are lit, and a blessing is said over two loaves of bread (*Hallot*), in memory of the double portion of manna that the Jews in the wilderness received on the Friday. The Sabbath is brought to a close on the Saturday evening, at the appearance of the first three stars, with *Havdalah*, the "separation" ceremony, recited over a cup of wine; breathing in the fragrance of the sweet-smelling spices (*Bessamim*), permits the sweetness of the Sabbath to last during the coming week. To prolong the ceremony further, a meal is served to bid the queen farewell (*melavveh Malkah*).

The ultimate aim of *Shabbat* is to enrich the "additional soul" (*neshamah yeterah*) that each Jew receives on the Sabbath, through what the prophet Isaiah (58: 13–14) calls "a day of joy". In this spirit, three celebratory meals are eaten, (*shalosh se'udot*), with abundant food cooked the previous day, enlivened by singing and animated discussion of the Torah. There is also time for study and rest during the course of the day, as well as for Synagogue services.

Cup for sanctification of the wine, *Kiddush*
Augsburg, c. 1700
Engraved, embossed silver gilt
13 x 8.4 cm
Strauss collection,
Rothschild donation
On long-term loan
from the Musée national
du Moyen Âge, Paris
D.98.4.89

Spice Tower, *Bessamim*
Austria, 18th century
Filigree silver
and enamelled plaques
H. 30 cm
Strauss collection,
Rothschild donation
On long-term loan
from the Musée national
du Moyen Âge, Paris
D.98.4.94

Learning

The Jews believe it is vitally important to teach the Torah to their children as the only way of ensuring that tradition will live on. The Talmud distinguishes between the *talmid hakham*, the scholar, and the *'am ha'aretz*, the ignoramus, introducing a hierarchy based on learning. From the third century, the communities living in Babylon established the *Yeshivah*, a generic term referring either to a teacher with whom students lived and studied, or an actual institution, with its own procedures, rules and customs. In North Africa and Spain, there is evidence of the existence of *Yeshivot* from the eighth century. The movement spread to Italy, the south and then the north of France, and then to northern, central and eastern Europe. Every city, however small, founded a *Yeshivah* that it administered and financed, and whose students it housed. What made the *Yeshivah* different was the students' desire to study for the sake of studying, *lishma*. The subject studied and the teaching methods tended to be virtually identical, whatever the place or time. The text studied was the Talmud. The students worked in pairs, *Havruta*, and prepared the text which was to form the basis for the teacher's lesson. The latter, who assumed that his students had understood the passage, would then discuss it and give an analysis (*hiddush*). The ultimate aim was to compare different passages, identify possible contradictions between them and finally focus on the consistency of the texts studied by producing a closely-argued semantic analysis, formulating new concepts, highlighting a particularly insightful reading or even by correcting the lesson: *girsa*. In the *Yeshivot* of Eastern Europe, from the sixteenth century, the emphasis was on *pilpul*, a particularly hair-splitting form of casuistry.

Portrait of Azriel Hildesheimer
(b. 1820, Halberstadt, d. 1899, Berlin)
Germany, c. 1890
Oil on canvas
55 x 46.5 cm
Gift of Victor Klagsbald
MAHJ 96.1.1

Azriel Hildesheimer devoted his life to the reconciliation of Jewish tradition and modern culture, following in the footsteps of Moses Mendelssohn and the Jewish movement of the Enlightenment, the *Haskalah*. Appointed a rabbi in 1851, at Eisenstadt, in Austria, he gave his *Yeshivah* a new dimension. The influence of his teaching, which integrated modernist thinking and philology into the orthodox perspective, placed him at the centre of the debate between Reform and ultra-orthodox Jews. Appointed a rabbi in Berlin in 1869, he became leader of the German Neo-orthodox movement alongside Samson Raphael Hirsch. He also encouraged the Reform trend in his fight against the growing anti-Semitism in Germany. He became involved in the Jews' defence organisation the *Hilfsverein*, particularly at the time of the pogroms in Russia in the 1880s, and gave his active support to the Lovers of Zion movement (*Hovevei Zion*) and the Jewish community in Palestine, the *Yishuv*.

Alm box
Central Europe, 1804
Engraved silver
9 x 8.5 cm
Gift of Louis Lille
Gift of the Musée d'Art juif de Paris
MAHJ 2002.1.767

Tzedakah

The first meaning of charity is expressed in Hebrew by the term *Tzedakah*, which comes from the word *Tzedek* ("justice"). The Talmud makes a distinction between *Tzedakah* and charity in the wider sense, *Gemilut Hasadim*, which includes help and assistance and the time devoted to others.

The early legislative forms of *Tzedakah* were the cyclical abolition of debts and the agrarian laws forcing landowners to leave the corners of their fields and the grain that escaped the harvest for the poor.

This controlling of wealth was secondary to concern for the poor. The traditional Jewish community had numerous charitable societies to provide relief for those in need and to help out in various circumstances: burying the poor, assisting travellers, paying the ransoms of hostages and providing daily meals for the needy.

The Days of Awe

The Jewish year begins with the solemn Days of Awe (*Yamim Noraim*), when judgement and repentance are paramount.

The festival of *Rosh ha-Shanah*, or New Year, is celebrated on the 1st and 2nd of Tishri, the seventh month in the Biblical calendar. This festival, which is one of the three "sacred assemblies" described in Leviticus (23:2-8), has three other names: "the Day of Judgment", when, according to the *Mishnah*, humanity is brought before God; the "Day of the *Shofar*", for the blowing of *Shofar* (ram's horn) accompanies the prayers, encouraging repentance (*Teshuvah*), and the "Day of Remembrance" (*Yom ha-Zikaron*), in commemoration of the Creation. Tradition introduces the symbolic notion of the Book of Life and the Book of Death, recording each individual's actions and the divine pronouncement as to their fate.

The verdict is not truly sealed until the Day of Atonement, *Yom Kippur*, celebrated after the ten days of atonement on 10 Tishri, by a fast and prayers of repentance lasting more than twenty-four hours. It is the "Day of Reckoning", the culmination of ten days of repentance. On the eve of the festival, different communities participate in various symbolic expiatory rituals: purification in the ritual bath, contrition rites, expiatory sacrifice and giving to the poor.

The services, punctuated by confessions and prayers, begin in the evening with the profound *Kol Nidre* prayer, which includes the whole congregation and nullifies hasty vows. They end the following evening with the closing service, *Ne'ilah* which takes place with the doors of the Ark open, and seals the destiny of human beings. One last long blast from the *Shofar* signals the end of the ceremony.

In some communities, many worshippers spend the day on their feet, keeping a vow of silence, saying only their prayers. The men wear a white shroud-like gown as a symbol of mourning and purification.

The traditional Sephardi world

Since Roman times, *Sefarad* has been the Hebrew word for the Iberian peninsula, and, strictly speaking, the Sephardim are descendants of the Jews who lived in Spain and Portugal before the expulsions of 1492 and 1497 and who, refusing to convert to satisfy the Catholic Monarchs, spread out to other Western European countries, but particularly to the Balkans, the near East and North Africa. By association – and in fact this is historically incorrect – all the Jews from the Maghreb or from the Near and Middle East are also called Sephardim – including those who are not of Judeo-Spanish origin.

The liturgical traditions of the Sephardim go back to the days of Babylonian Judaism in the early centuries. Throughout history, the Sephardi communities have remained united around observance of religious law, through the adherence to practices set down in meticulous detail in the sixteenth century by Joseph Caro in the *Shulḇan 'Aruch*, and fidelity to customary practices. Even today, they have been only slightly affected by doctrinal controversies and ideological upheavals, unlike the Jews of Europe.

Between the Muslim conquest and the end of the sixteenth century, the Sephardi communities displayed an intense cultural vitality, especially in the fields of literature – sacred and secular, Hebrew, Judeo-Spanish, and in the languages of their countries of residence –, philosophy, medicine and Jewish studies. This "Golden Age" was followed by a long period of stagnation, especially in North Africa, where most Jews were reduced to the status of *dhimmi*, both protected and inferior, and continued to live in the closed society of the *mellah* or the *hara* – equivalent to the European ghettos –, deprived of any real interaction with the outside world, and suffered from harsh material living conditions.

During the twentieth century, the Sephardi communities have undergone huge demographic and geographic changes. Some

Jewish woman and her daughter
Tunis, late 19th century
Albumen print
27.8 x 21 cm
MAHJ ph/40

of them – such as the community of Salonica – were wiped out by the Holocaust. Furthermore, there was massive emigration in the second half of the century, and many Sephardim went to the United States, Canada, Latin America and Israel, where they now make up the majority of the population.

Torah finials, *Rimmonim*
Morocco, 19th century
Silver, cloisonné enamel,
and traces of gilded silver
26.5 x 6 cm
MAHJ 91.2.4

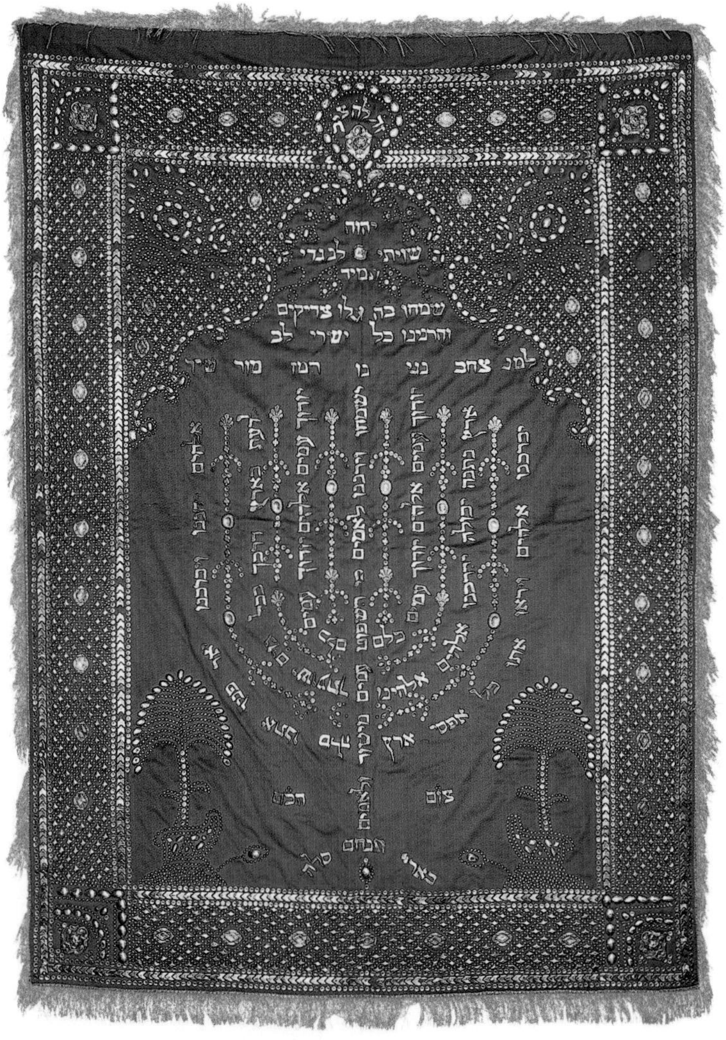

Ark curtain, *Parokhet*
Turkey, 19th century
Velvet and silver decorations, sewn on
188 x 132 cm
Camondo donation
On long-term loan from the Musée national du Moyen Âge, Paris
D.98.4.135

At the centre of the frame in the shape of a *Mihrab* is a *Menorah* whose seven branches are formed by the words of Psalm 67 made up of cut out silver letters. Embroidered on the top of the *Mihrab* are the initials of the verse "This is the gate of the Lord; the righteous shall enter therein" (Psalm 118: 20), a reminder that the Ark, like the *Mihrab*, symbolises the gates to heaven.

Torah case and scroll, *Tik*
Ottoman Empire, 1860
Wood, engraved and embossed silver, gazelle skin
86 x 21 cm
Camondo donation
On long-term loan from the Musée national du Moyen Âge, Paris
D.98.4.120

This richly adorned *Tik* (cylindrical case), is a traditional shape specific to the Near East and Ottoman Empire. Inside the domed top are two inscriptions. On the right, the verses from Deuteronomy (4: 44), Leviticus (26: 46, slightly modified) and Proverbs (2: 18). The case belonged, as we are informed by the inscription on the left, "to the notable, revered, magnificent lord, the influential prince in Israel, R. Señor Camondo of the Camondo lineage." Abraham de Camondo (1785-1873), banker and leader of the Jewish community of Constantinople, was a man who enjoyed great influence among the Ottoman sultans and also with the Austrian and Italian governments. The King of Italy gave him the title of Count, in recognition of his philanthropic activities.

The production of gold thread in Morocco

In North Africa, the manufacture of gold thread was traditionally in the hands of Jewish craftsmen, as was embroidery, commerce, the production of braid, etc. In Morocco, these crafts developed mainly in Fez.

Before being industrialised, the manufacturing process for gold thread was made up of different stages, each one involving a different craft. The purchasing of the raw materials and the sale of the finished products was the job of the owners, *ma'allemin skalli*, who entrusted the work to craftsmen and supervised its organisation.

The gold, bought in different forms, was given to the beaters, who transformed it into gold leaf. After checking the purity of the metal, the next step was the gilding of silver sticks: heated on a clay stove, they were then rolled in gold leaf and browned; an initial wire-drawing produced a rope of gilded silver 7.5 mm in diameter.

This rope was given to specialist wire-drawers who reduced it to a diameter of 1 millimetre, after which the owners took the gold thread, coiled round reels, to the rollers who made it into foil.

At the same time, the owners gave the silk to the spinners to twist. This aspect of the work was entrusted to Jewish women who were single or from a modest background.

The gold thread manufacturers, strictly speaking, were the spinners: their job was to roll the gold foil around the spun silk, which was the final stage in the production of gold thread.
This very ancient technique survived until around 1920, when some owners began to import foil from Europe, and then the machines for making the foil and rolling it around the silk.

Woman's headdress
Algeria, 19th century
Velvet, gold thread, metallic braid and sequins
14.5 x 16 cm
Gift of Georges Aboucaya, in memory of Colette Aboucaya-Spira
MAHJ 91.12.23

The conical headdress, *chechia*, of red velvet, entirely covered in embroidery of gold and metallic braid and sequins, was fastened under the chin with a strap. It was part of the wedding outfit. This type of headdress developed from the *hennin*, or steeple headdress, worn in Europe in the Middle Ages, was unknown in Algeria before the 18th century. The first description of it is dated 1816 when the Egyptian interpreter, Abraham Salamé visited Algeria.

Ceremonial dress,
Kswa el Kbirah
Tetuan, Morocco,
late 19th century
Silk velvet, gold braid
and lining of printed cotton
111 x 329 cm
Gift of Sete Guetta,
in memory of her father,
Raphael Benazeraf
MAHJ 96.2.1

The *Kswa el Kbirah*, also called "berberisca", is the ceremonial dress of the Jewish city dweller, and is part of a bride's dowry. This costume is made up of three parts, the skirt, the bodice and the embroidered velvet bolero. It can also have a silk and gold braid belt, and mousseline sleeves, not shown here. It is typical of the big coastal cities of northern Morocco and only the colours and the decoration vary from one city to another. The one thing that is inseparable from the ceremonial dress is the headdress. The Talmud in fact forbids married women from displaying their hair. It must be hidden right to the roots. In Morocco this precept led to the widest variety of wigs and hair styles. Rural headdresses are the most original. In many Moroccan families, both urban and rural, the ceremonial dress is handed down from mother to daughter. Girls don it on the eve of their wedding for the henna ceremony. It has become a sort of national dress.

Félix Barrias
(b. 1822, Paris, d. 1907, Paris)
Woman with *Hennin*
1890
Oil on canvas
41.5 x 33 cm
Gift of Georges Aboucaya
in memory of
Colette Aboucaya-Spira
MAHJ 91.12.38

A graduate of the École des Beaux-Arts, Félix Barrias first exhibited at the Paris Salon in 1840. In 1844, he was awarded the Prix de Rome. In addition to large-scale historical compositions, featuring in particular Greek and Roman history, he also produced decorative works (Hôtel-de-Ville, foyer of the Opéra de Paris, 1874) and religious paintings (churches of Saint-Eustache and Trinité). During the course of his long career, he devoted himself to the illustration of literary works (Virgil, Horace, Molière ...) and left several portraits, including this *Woman with* Hennin. The woman's dress, with an embroidered plastron (bodice) worn over a wide-sleeved shirt and embroidered *Hennin*, is typical of the Jewish women of Constantine.

Jacket
Ottoman Empire, 19th century
Velvet, gold thread
60 x 178 cm
Gift of Georges Aboucaya
in memory of
Colette Aboucaya-Spira
MAHJ 91.12.24

This black velvet jacket, sumptuously decorated with a gold floral design, gold thread embroidery and braid, was worn by town-dwelling Jewish women in the Ottoman Empire.
The pattern is made up of five elements: the bud, the flower, the leaf, the stem and the shoot, either separately or together, the stems forming the basis of the design. The same motifs can be found in Ottoman architecture, painting, bookbinding, manuscript illuminations and textiles.

Alfred Dehodencq
(b. 1822, Paris, d. 1882, Paris)
Jewish festival in Tetuan
Paris, c. 1858
Oil on canvas
120 x 90 cm
Acquired with the help of a subsidy from the FRAM of the Île-de-France
MAHJ 95.13.1

Alfred Dehodencq left Paris after the revolution of 1848. He travelled in Spain, where he married. Between 1853 and 1863, he set sail from Cadiz on a number of voyages to Morocco, which held a profound fascination for him. He showed a keen interest in the Jewish population, observing their rites and customs, and making the Jews the subject of his paintings, as did Théodore Chassériau and Eugène Delacroix in particular. He produced numerous studies portraying a Morocco that is vibrant, intense, noisy and full of life. His stark, bright colours and the extensive use of black are suited to the violence of his subjects (*The Torture of the Thieves, The Execution of the Jewess, The Pasha's Justice*). This painting depicts an annual procession of the Jews of Tetuan, who were allowed to parade through the streets in memory of a service rendered. The procession, preceded by two musicians, is emerging from the *Mellah*, whose gate is visible in the background.

ÉDIT DU ROI,

PORTANT

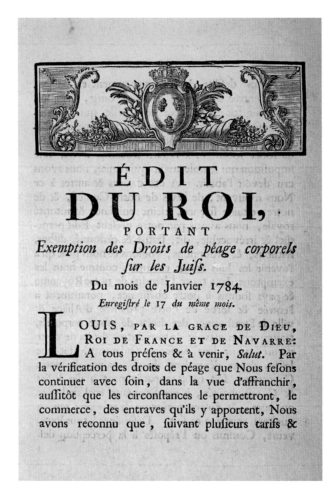

Exemption des Droits de péage corporels ſur les Juiſs.

Du mois de Janvier 1784.

Enregiſtré le 17 du même mois.

LOUIS, PAR LA GRACE DE DIEU, ROI DE FRANCE ET DE NAVARRE: A tous préſens & à venir, *Salut.* Par la vérification des droits de péage que Nous feſons continuer avec ſoin, dans la vue d'affranchir, auſſitôt que les circonſtances le permettront, le commerce, des entraves qu'ils y apportent, Nous avons reconnu que, ſuivant pluſieurs tarifs &

Emancipation: the French model

Royal Edict, granting exemption from *péage corporel* (body tax) on the Jews
Colmar, Decker's house,
17 January 1784
Printed notice
24.8 x 20.5 cm
MAHJ 91.2.1

Cerf Berr was the representative of the Jewish "nation" in Alsace. He worked tirelessly to have the restrictions on the Jews lifted. In 1780, he commissioned the Berlin Jewish philosopher Moses Mendelssohn to write a memorandum in favour of the emancipation of the Jews. Mendelssohn thought it more appropriate to give this task to Christian Wilhelm von Dohm, military councellor to the King of Prussia, whose work was translated into French by Mirabeau. Its publication, in 1782, was rapidly followed

By the end of Louis XVI's reign, there were more than 40,000 Jews in France, of whom 25,000 lived in Alsace, 7,500 in Metz and in Lorraine, and some 4,000 in the south-west, between Bordeaux and Bayonne. A few hundred Jews also lived in Paris. As for the 1,500 Jews then living in the *carrières* (Jewish quarters) of Avignon and the Comtat, they did not belong to the kingdom of France but were dependent on the Papal states.

In France, the ideas expounded by the Enlightenment, in particular tolerance and the advocacy of reason, won the support of liberal noblemen, the bourgeoisie and various Jewish notables influenced by the writings of the Berlin philosopher Moses Mendelssohn.

In 1787, the year where civil equality was granted to Protestants, an essay competition on the question: "Are there any ways of making the Jews of France happier and more useful?" was set by the Société Royale des Arts et Sciences in Metz. The three joint prize-winners, including the Abbé Grégoire, pointed out that the economic emancipation of the Jews and the elimination of the restrictive measures imposed on them would permit their full integration.

During the French National Assembly of July 1788 opinions remained split on the Jewish question: not everybody wanted to see the Jews enjoying full civil rights.

The Declaration of the Rights of Man adopted on 26 August 1789 put an end to any form of discrimination between citizens, but the Assembly was still divided, as were the Jews themselves. The "Portuguese" Jews of Bordeaux and Bayonne, who were often well-off, wanted to hold on to their privileges and were reluctant to be grouped together with the "German" Jews of eastern France, who were less affluent and more traditionalist. Meanwhile, the Jewish minority that had temporarily settled in Paris made a lone representation to the Assembly to defend its rights.

by the abolition of the *péage corporel* (a body tax on entering cities) to which the Jews had been subjected since the Middle Ages. The Royal Decree was written in the following terms: "The Jews are subject to a corporal tax which ranks them alongside animals; and as it is repulsive to our sentiments that we extend to all our subjects to allow a single one of them to remain subject to a tax which seems to debase humanity, we believe we should abolish it." This measure marked the beginning of improvements in the legal status of the Jews in France on the eve of the Revolution.

The decree of 28 January 1790 made the Portuguese Jews the first "active citizens". The decree emancipating all Jews was finally adopted twenty months later, on 27 September 1791, after a bitter political struggle. The Jews were now equal to other citizens, with equal rights and duties, and their religious practice belonged strictly to the private sphere. This was the model for French Jews, who were able to combine fidelity to their roots with patriotism, setting the example for most of Western Europe.

Despite a few ambiguous measures introduced by Napoleon I so as not to antagonise the conservative elements – such as the *décret infâme* of 1808 –, the integration of the Jews and confirmation of their political rights continued under the Second Republic and the Second Empire. But it was the Third Republic that saw the birth of true "Franco-Judaism", marked by the Jews' fervent attachment to France, "the home of the rights of man".

During the same period, however, anti-Semitism gained ground: Édouard Drumont, for example, poured out his hatred in his book entitled *La France juive* (Jewish France), and in his newspaper, *La Libre Parole* (Free Speech). Autumn 1894 saw the eruption of the Dreyfus Affair, which split France into two camps: the partisans of justice and tolerance on the one hand, and the supporters of extreme nationalism and rejection on the other.

Despite the pardon granted in 1899 to Captain Dreyfus – whose innocence was officially recognised in 1906 –, the Jews of France were vulnerable and worried, aware of the fact that a not insignificant section of the political class and of public opinion remained hostile to their integration. Whether they were of French origin or immigrants from Eastern Europe, (from the 1880s), they still remained profoundly patriotic, as was demonstrated by their participation in World War I, during which more than 7,000 Jews died on the battlefields.

Moses Mendelssohn and the *Haskalah*

The *Haskalah* movement advocated Judaism's entry into modernity and sought to create the emergence of a new Jew, emancipated from the social, professional and linguistic ghetto. A key figure of this movement was the philosopher Moses Mendelssohn, who tried to reconcile Jewish tradition with the rationalist philosophy of the German Enlightenment (*Aufklärung*). The author of a number of philosophical works, including *Phädon, oder über die Unsterblichkeit der Seele* (*Phaedo, or on the Immortality of the Soul*) published in 1767, he started working on a German translation of the Bible, published in Hebrew lettering, accompanied by the original text and the *Bi'ur*, a critical commentary based on traditional exegesis. For Mendelssohn and his colleagues, the rationalist approach to religion and intellectual revival were closely bound up with the struggle for the political emancipation of the Jews. From 1770, on numerous occasions he acted as arbitrator between the Jews and the Prussian authorities and those of other principalities. He inspired the memorandum in favour of improving the status of French Jews. He was also one of the founders of the first Jewish schools where teaching was in German, the *Jüdische Freyschule*, which opened in Berlin in 1778. His political and religious positions earned him some fierce enemies among the Orthodox Jewish community. All the same, he was the most admired Jew of his day, and Gotthold Ephraim Lessing made him the eponymous hero of *Nathan der Weise*.

Moses Mendelssohn
(b. 1729, Dessau, d. 1786, Berlin)
Johann Friedrich Bause
(b. 1738, Halle, Saxony,
d. 1814, Weimar), based
on a portrait by Anton Graff
Leipzig, 1772
Etching
27.5 x 20.2 cm
MAHJ 94.1.14

The Consistories

After 1808, the new organisation of the practice of Judaism was based on a network of Consistories. A synagogue and a Consistory were established in all the territories conquered by Napoleon's armies, and in every *département* with at least 2,000 Jews.

Each Consistory was led by a " chief rabbi " assisted by another rabbi and laymen appointed by the notables and approved by the civil authorities. Their task was to supervise the practice of the Jewish religion and at the same time to instil patriotic values. At the head of this administrative system was the Central Consistory in Paris.

Portrait of the Chief Rabbi David Sintzheim
France, early 19th century
Oil on canvas
32.5 x 24 cm
MAHJ 90.2.1

David Sintzheim was born in Trier in 1745. Trained by his father, a rabbi at Niedernai, he was a learned Talmud scholar. In 1786, he took over the directorship of the *Yeshivah* founded by his brother-in-law, Cerf Beer, at Bischheim, before being appointed rabbi in Strasbourg, in 1792. The political condition of the Jews was central to his concerns: he attended the National Constitutive Assembly in August 1789 as the Alsace delegate in order to demand the emancipation of the Jews of eastern France. He requested the protection of the National Assembly and protested against the acts of violence perpetrated in July 1789 in Alsace and Lorraine. His reputation as a scholar and man of commitment preceded him when he went to Paris to sit at the Assembly of Jewish Notables. Appointed president of the Great Sanhedrin, he became the Chief Rabbi of the Central Consistory in 1808. This portrait appears to have been painted during Sintzheim's lifetime. David Sintzheim is depicted in ecclesiastical dress. His hat is not the traditional headgear, but a special cocked hat reminiscent both of the high priest's mitre and of the horned portrayal of Moses. This dunce's cap, laden with negative connotations, could reflect Napoleon's contempt for the Jews.

Édouard Moyse
(Nancy, 1827- Nancy, 1908)
The Great Sanhedrin
France, 1867
Oil on canvas
53 x 97 cm
MAHJ 94.9.1

Édouard Moyse and Édouard Brandon were the first to depict Jewish life in France and defining moments of Jewish history. Moyse's paintings include *The Heretics before the Tribunal of the Inquisition at Seville in* 1481 (Louviers Museum), *The Talmud Lesson* (Musée historique lorrain, Nancy), *Elevation of the Law* (Synagogue in rue Buffault, Paris). This work is a highly developed sketch of the painting in the Nancy Musée des Beaux-Arts. This was one of the first major scenes of Jewish life painted by a Jewish artist to be exhibited at the Salon.

The Great Sanhedrin

In the belief that making the Jews citizens was not sufficient to make them "useful", Napoleon demanded guarantees from them and insisted they be governed by French law. For this purpose he brought together, in July 1806, an Assembly of Jewish Notables who had to answer twelve specific questions on the relationship between religious law and civil law, the loyalty of the Jews to the country, the jurisdiction of the rabbis and usury. Then, to ratify their replies, he convened a Great Sanhedrin, modelled on that of Jerusalem, with seventy-one members, two thirds of whom were rabbis. They sat between the 9 February and 9 March 1807. After March 1807, the Assembly of Jewish Notables continued its work, and it was on the basis of its conclusions that Napoleon promulgated the Imperial Decrees of 1808 regarding the organisation of the Jewish religion.

Jean Lubin Vauzelle
(b. 1776, Angerville-la-Gâte,
d. 1837,?)
Interior of the synagogue at Bordeaux and its architect, A. Corcelles
Bordeaux, c. 1812
Oil on canvas and panels
98.8 x 109 cm
MAHJ 95.44.1

The building of monumental synagogues during the nineteenth century was one of the more visible aspects of the Jews' entry into the public arena. The architectural and stylistic choices expressed this new relationship with the city. Still rather discreet, the first synagogue of this period was inaugurated in Bordeaux, rue Causserouge, in 1812. It reflected the fashion for neo-classicism: a basilica shape with Greek ornamentation and Egyptian-style lamps. The decoration reflects a wish to cite as many Biblical references as possible. The architect, Corcelles, depicted here standing in the synagogue, took his inspiration for the highly original façade from the priest's mitre imposed by Napoleon on the Chief Rabbi of the Consistory. Destroyed by a fire in 1873, the synagogue was rebuilt in 1882, and fitted with exact replicas of the original furniture.

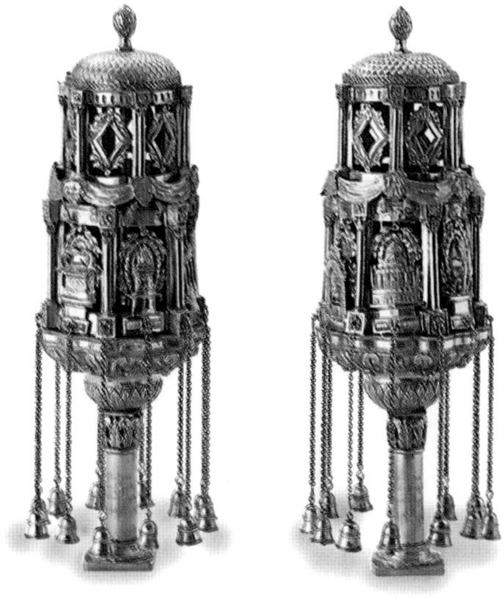

Torah finials, *Rimmonim*
Montauban, 1809-1819
Silver, embossed, chased and engraved
50 x 22 cm
Gift of Nestor and Éléonore Dreyfus, 1877
On long-term loan from the Paris Consistory
D.95.3.25.1-2

Édouard Brandon
(b. 1831, Paris, d. 1897, Paris)
The Sermon of the Fast of Av
Paris, 1867
Oil on canvas stuck to wood
21.5 x 46.5 cm
On long-term loan from
the Musée du Louvre, Paris
D.94.5.1

Édouard Brandon belonged to an old Sephardi family from Bayonne. A contemporary of the Impressionists, together with whom he exhibited in 1874, he concentrated on Jewish themes in his work, especially Sephardi worship. A day of mourning, fasting and abstinence, the 9 Av (*Tish'ah be-Av*), celebrated here in the Portuguese synagogue of Amsterdam, commemorates the destruction of the first and of the second Temple of Jerusalem, and also symbolises all the suffering of the Jews in exile. The sermon is given here by the famous Talmud scholar, David de Jahacob Lopez Cardozo (1808-1890).

Jewish Themes in nineteenth-century painting

From the middle of the nineteenth century, the first Jewish artists able to enjoy the status of "professional artist" depicted the Jewish world in many different ways, depending on the cultural and social contexts in which they worked.

In Central Europe and Germany, where the Jewish communities had become rapidly assimilated, two artists rose to prominence among an integrated bourgeoisie for whom they evoked a traditional way of life that was dying out: Moritz Oppenheim (1800–1882), a genre painter patronised by the Rothschilds, whose *Bilder aus dem altjüdischen familienleben* (Family Scenes from Jewish Life of Former Days) were very popular, and Isidore Kaufmann (1853–1921), a Hungarian Jew who had settled in Vienna, and who haunted the Jewish quarters of Galicia and Ukraine to capture moments of *shtetl* life.

In France, the works of Édouard Brandon (1831–1897) and Édouard Moyse (1827–1908), illustrated landmarks in Jewish history – from the Spanish Inquisition to the setting up of the Consistories under Napoleon. Depicting the heyday of Jewish life and leading French Jews, they celebrate a new identity, that of the French Jew.

In a world shattered by crises, pogroms and also struggles within Judaism, Russian and Polish artists did not have the freedom to think about their identity in religious terms or even to devote themselves to idealising the past. The powerful dramatic tone of Samuel Hirszenberg's works (*The Jewish Cemetery, The Black Banner*) – and the painting by Maurycy Minkowski (1881-1930), *After the Pogrom*, reflect the growing awareness among the Jews of Russia and Poland of their history, and the identity struggles that marked the turn of the century.

Portrait of the Wandering Jew
France, 18th century
End-grained wood,
hand coloured on laid paper
44 x 30.2 cm
Donated by M. and Mme Harburger
MAHJ 91.4.1

The Christian legend of the Wandering Jew was a widespread iconographic and literary theme in European countries up until the twentieth century. This figure of the Jew, generally called Ahasver, who, having refused to help Jesus on the Way of the Cross, is condemned to wander for ever, inspired a mixture of horror and compassion. Late eighteenth century folk-art images and French and Rhenish carved figurines display clear differences to the anti-Jewish caricatures of the mid-nineteenth century. Until the beginning of the nineteenth century, the images of the Wandering Jew usually showed a "venerable old man" with the features of a gentle pilgrim wanderer. The popularity of Épinal imagery, from the late eighteenth century, marked the transition from Christian anti-Judaism to anti-Semitism: now the Jew was portrayed with a hooked nose and often repugnant garb. The Jews were viewed as outsiders until the Revolution, and anti-Semitic phobia did not take hold until the integration of the Jews into the nation. Then they were portrayed with the characteristics that became the classic attributes of the Jew in anti-Semitic illustrations, from the Dreyfus Affair to the exhibition of the Grand Rex, under the Vichy government.

Jules Jean Antoine
Lecomte du Noüy
(b. 1842, Paris, d. 1923, Paris)
Portrait of Adolphe Crémieux (1796-1880)
Paris, 1878
Oil on canvas
121 x 120 cm
On long-term loan from
the Musée d'Orsay, Paris
R.F. 1968-11

Isaac Adolphe Crémieux devoted his life to the liberal cause and to the defence of Jewish rights all over the world. Born in 1796, in Nîmes, into an old family from the Comtat Venaissin, he was the first Jewish pupil to gain admission to the Lycée impérial in Paris. A lawyer, he was called to the bar in Nîmes, where he refused to take the *more judaico* oath (sworn on the Torah) imposed on Jews involved in legal proceedings with non-Jews. His battle led to the abolition of the oath in 1846. He moved to Paris in 1830 and became a member of the Central Consistory, of which he was appointed president in 1843; in 1840 he played a crucial part in the Damas affair (an accusation of ritual murder), alongside Moses Montefiore. He was elected to the Chamber of Deputies in 1842, and served as Minister of Justice in the provisional government of 1848-1849. Crémieux withdrew from political life under the Second Empire, and devoted himself to Jewish affairs. He was elected president of the Alliance Israélite Universelle in 1864, and worked for that organisation until his death, defending oppressed Jewish communities around the world. He returned to government in 1870. His name remains associated with the decree that gave French nationality to the Jews of Algeria, in 1870. He was made a life senator in 1875.

The Jews of Alsace

There has been an uninterrupted Jewish presence in Alsace since the twelfth century, in spite of discrimination. Over the centuries, Ashkenazi communities thrived in rural areas; the Jews were an integral part of the Alsace landscape, even though until the nineteenth century they were relegated to a marginal status which banned Jews from towns, prevented them from owning land, and confined them to occupations generally held in contempt such as pedlar, small money-lender or trader.

Key features of Jewish life were a close-knit community, piety strongly rooted in everyday life, and a language, Judeo-Alsatian. Eminent figures such as Rabbi Joselman of Rosheim, during the Renaissance period, contributed to its rich development. This rural Judaism gave rise to colourful characters such as the beadle, the livestock merchant and the pedlar, as portrayed in Alphonse Lévy's works which swing between nostalgia and satire.

In the nineteenth century, community life was severely disrupted by changes in the status of Jews resulting from the Revolution and the advent of the Empire. The Jews resisted in a bid to hold on to their autonomy, but the introduction of surnames, the establishment of Consistories and mandatory conscription decreed by Napoleon I ultimately forced the Jews of Alsace to conform to French economic and legal structures.

Once all professions were open to the Jews, some embraced a military career, others became wealthy through commerce and industry, some chose the liberal professions and others went into academia. They moved into the cities such as Strasbourg, Metz, Nancy and Colmar, and many settled in Paris.

Enjoying their new freedom and proud of the achievements of emancipation, the Jews became fiercely patriotic. After the annexation of Alsace and Lorraine by the Germans following the war of 1870, many Jews chose to leave Alsace for Normandy, Épinal, Lyon and Paris, or to emigrate to America or North Africa. Despite the Germanisation of the communities that stayed behind, most of them welcomed the handing back of Alsace and Lorraine to France in 1918.

Entrenched in rural life and tradition, part of the Jewish population of Alsace remained scattered in numerous villages until World War II. Senior Jewish figures and Rabbis from Alsace have left an indelible mark on contemporary French Jewish history.

Alphonse Lévy (b. 1843, Marmoutier, d. 1918, Alger)
Yom Kippur
France, late 19th century
Lithograph
43.5 x 59 cm
Gift of the Musée d'Art juif de Paris
MAHJ 2002.1.91

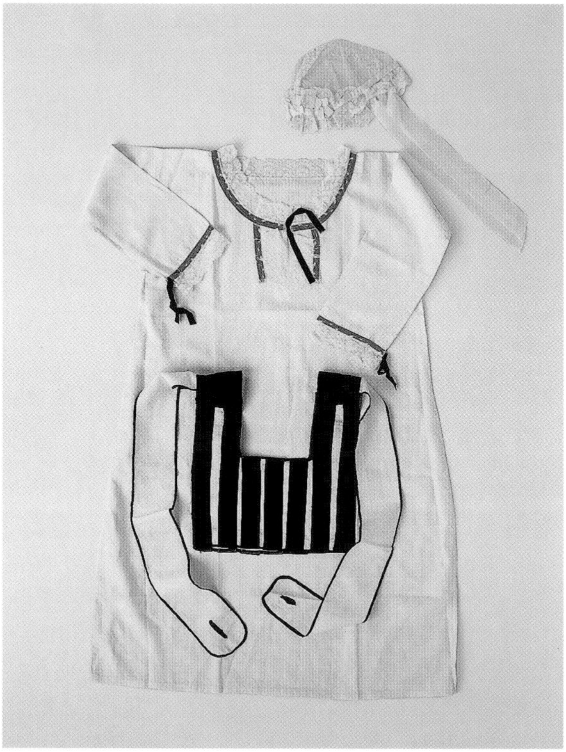

Burial shroud, *Sargeness*
Alsace, c. 1903
Ivory white linen,
lace and black ribbon
119 x 81 cm
Gift of Mme Julien Lévy,
in memory of her mother,
Mme Moyse
MAHJ 95.35.1

Death

The Jews believe in the resurrection of the dead with the coming of the Messiah. This belief has always been central to the Jewish religion, finding expression in the visions of the prophets, such as the one described in Daniel (12:2): "Many of those who sleep in the dust of the earth will wake, some to everlasting life, and some to the reproach of eternal abhorrence."

Preserving life and assisting the sick and the dying are fundamental duties and every Jewish community has its mutual benefit society, known as *Hevra Kaddisha*, whose members take on the duty of watching over and burying the dead, and comforting the bereaved. It is they who carry out the ritual washing of the deceased, putting on the simple white shroud (*sargeness*) and the *tallit*, if the departed is a man, and the burial. Then, the bereaved recite *Kaddish* over the grave, and the family and close relations rend their garments (*keriah*), to show their grief. The family observes a seven-day period of mourning (*shiv'ah)* – the first three days in silence – and receives daily visits from members of the community; the thirty days following the burial (*shloshim*) enable them to return to their normal routine while observing mourning in private.

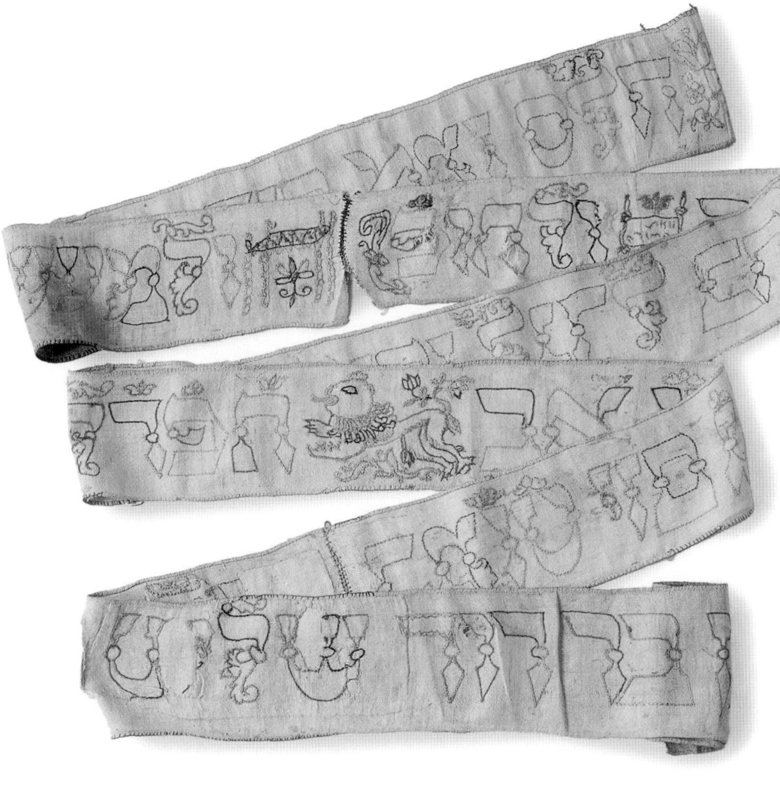

Torah binder, *Mappah*
Alsace, 1724
Embroidered linen
360 x 11 cm
Gift of Robert Nordman
MAHJ 90.1.37

"Levirate or barefoot marriage ceremony"
From the *Dictionnaire historique et critique de la Bible*
Augustin Calmet
Paris, 1730
Engraving on laid paper
32 x 20.5 cm
MAHJ 95.22.1

PLECHTIGHEIT VAN HET UYTTREKKEN DER SCHOE VAN DEN VOET VAN EENES MANS BROEDER.
Deuter. XXV. 7.8.9.

Levirate, or marriage between a widow and her husband's brother, if she is childless, is a commandment: "the first son she bears shall perpetuate the dead brother's name so that it may not be blotted out from Israel." Deuteronomy, 25:6. Deuteronomy also lays down a ritual permitting the dead man's brother to be released from this duty, and likewise his widow. This rite is called *Halitzah*, from the Hebrew *halatz*, "removing one's sandals".
This ceremony must be performed before a tribunal made up of five rabbis.
The widow reads the verse from Deuteronomy concerning Levirate, then she removes her brother-in-law's right sandal. She spits in his face and repeats the following formula: "Thus we requite the man who will not build up his brother's family!".

Shoe for the *Halitzah* ceremony
Hegenheim, Alsace, 18th century
Leather
15 x 28 cm
Gift of Robert Nordman
MAHJ 95.36.1

Alphonse Lévy
(b. 1843, Marmoutier,
d. 1918, Alger, 1918)
"Evening prayer"
(Prayer to the moon)
France, pre-1883
Oil on canvas
61 x 43 cm
Gift of the Musée d'Art juif
de Paris
MAHJ 2002.1.637

Once a pupil of Jean-Léon Gérôme, then a caricaturist for the satirical paper *La Lune*, Alphonse Lévy began painting Jewish subjects from 1890. He illustrated two books, *La Vie juive* by Léon Cahun (1886), and *Contes juifs* by Sacher-Masoch (1888). He then embarked on a series of lithographs, *Scènes familiales juives*, with a preface by Bernard Lazare, published in 1903. The subject of his paintings is the rural Jewish population of Alsace, where he was born. His portrayal of this traditional world trying to get to grips with modernity, while not devoid of nostalgia, refuses to idealise it, unlike Moritz Oppenheim in Frankfurt whose *Family Scenes from Jewish Life of Former Days* were hugely popular among a bourgeoisie that was becoming assimilated. Success continued to elude him and he left for Algeria, where the population, especially the Jews, inspired him to produce countless sketches, drawings and paintings.

The Dreyfus Collection

The grandchildren of Captain Dreyfus have donated an archive of more than 3,000 documents to the Musée d'art and d'histoire du Judaïsme. These crucial pieces bear witness to Dreyfus' ordeal and to the solidarity of a family which put all its energy into proving the innocence of the convicted man. They include the order for him to be deported to Devil's Island, which a guard managed to keep and give to the Captain, the authorisations given to Lucie Dreyfus, on the île de Ré, to see her husband for the last time, and at Rennes to see him after five years' imprisonment, accompanied by the letter she wrote to him when they were reunited on that occasion; the original of the magnificent letter Dreyfus wrote to his wife on 31 July 1895, in which he described all his suffering, but said he would not allow himself to die until his innocence was recognised; two deeply moving letters from Mathieu Dreyfus, written the day after the Captain was stripped of his rank, urging Dreyfus to live and to fight, and promising to do his utmost to have him brought back, free and cleared of having committed any crime; the subpoena sent to Lucie Dreyfus for Zola's trial; the cablegram informing Dreyfus that his conviction had been quashed and the list of witnesses drawn up by the government commissioner for the Rennes trial; Dreyfus' comments on various statements given at the Rennes trial, written in prison and a copy of *Cinq Années de ma vie (Five Years of my Life)*, with handwritten corrections and notes.

The bulk of the collection is made up of more than 2,200 letters addressed to Lucie Dreyfus and to the Captain, during his imprisonment on Devil's Island and particularly during the least-known period of the Affair, between the second conviction, the pardon and Dreyfus' retirement.

The archives include numerous photographs, including some previously unpublished ones of the Rennes trial, as well as a splendid collection of postcards.

Émile Zola
(Paris, 1840- Paris, 1902)
"J'Accuse... !"
L'Aurore
Paris, 13 January 1898
Newsprint
64.8 x 46.9 cm
Gift of Georges Aboucaya
in memory of
Colette Aboucaya-Spira
MAHJ 96.33.4

Alfred Dreyfus
Carpentras, c. 1900
Photograph
Gift of Captain Dreyfus' grandchildren
MAHJ 97.17.58

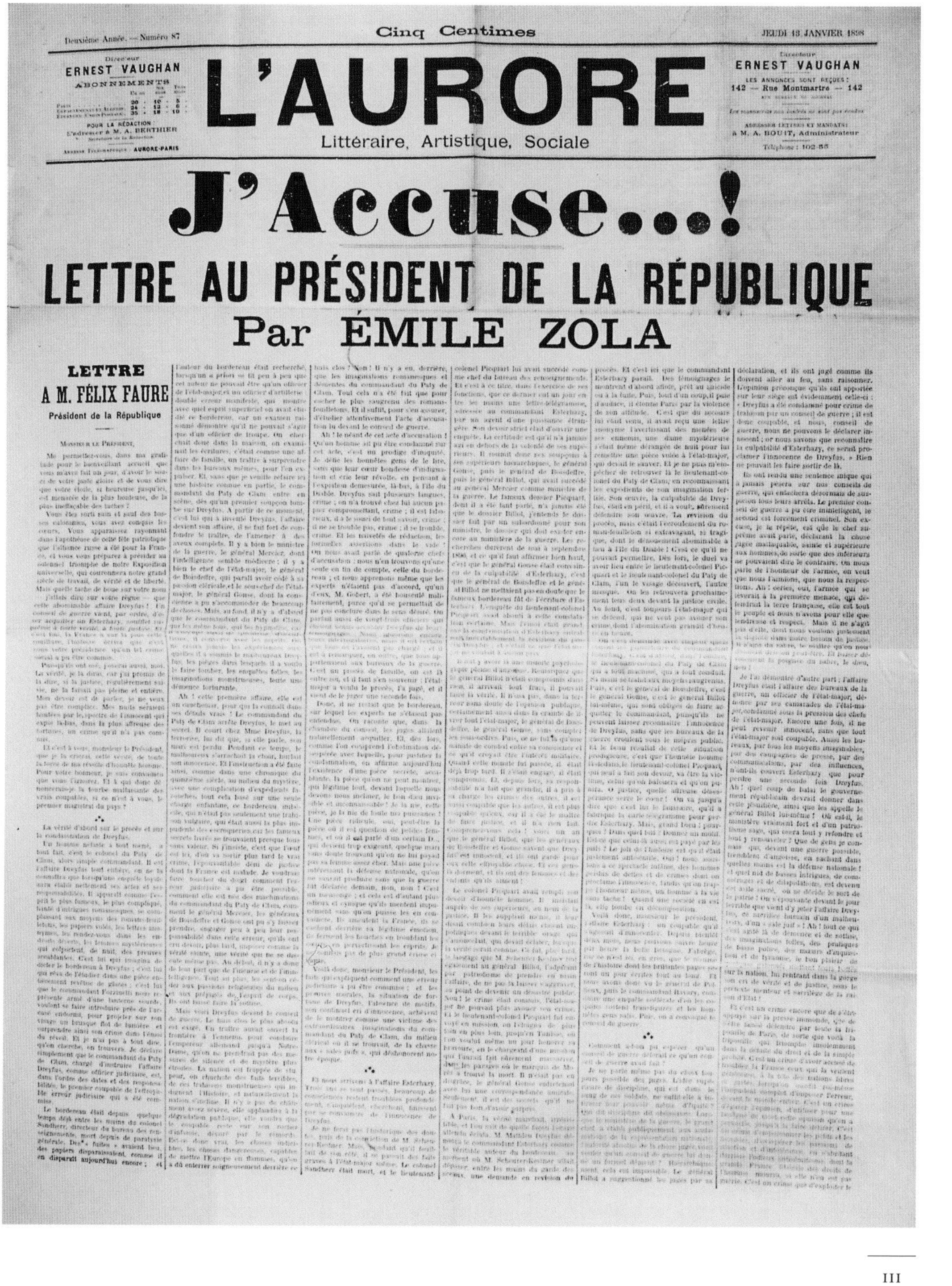
Deuxième Année. — Numéro 87

Cinq Centimes

JEUDI 13 JANVIER 1898

Directeur
ERNEST VAUGHAN
ABONNEMENTS

POUR LA RÉDACTION :
S'adresser à M. A. BERTHIER

AURORE-PARIS

L'AURORE

Littéraire, Artistique, Sociale

Directeur
ERNEST VAUGHAN
LES ANNONCES SONT REÇUES :
142 — Rue Montmartre — 142

ADRESSER LETTRES ET MANDATS
à M. A. BOUIT, Administrateur
Téléphone : 102-88

J'Accuse...!

LETTRE AU PRÉSIDENT DE LA RÉPUBLIQUE

Par ÉMILE ZOLA

LETTRE
A M. FÉLIX FAURE
Président de la République

Monsieur le Président,

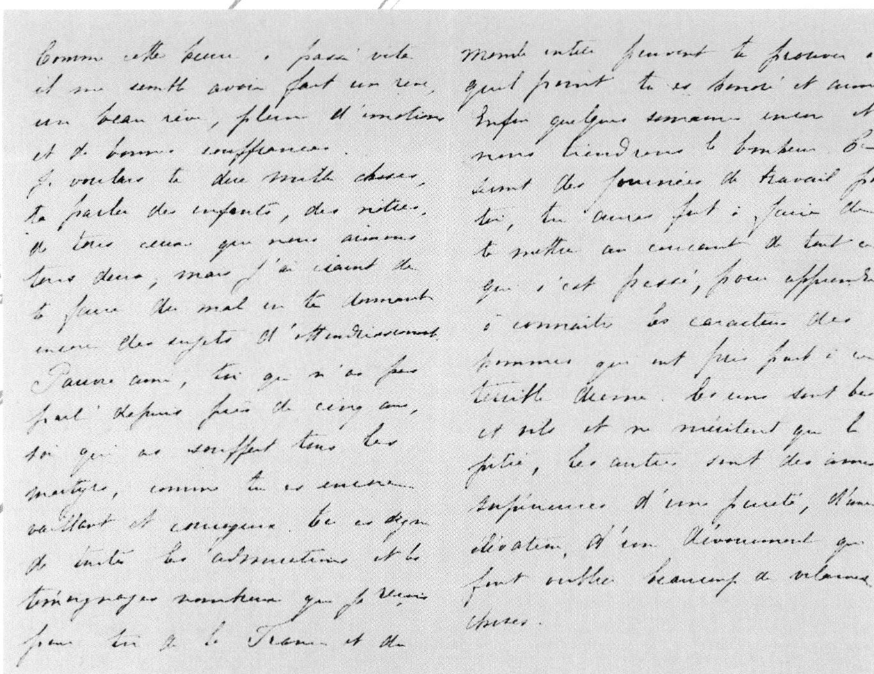

Comme cette heure a passé vite
il me semble avoir fait un rêve,
un beau rêve, plein d'émotion
et de bonne espérance.
Je voulais te dire mille choses,
te parler des enfants, des nôtres,
de tous ceux que nous aimons
tous deux, mais j'ai craint de
te faire du mal en te donnant
encore des sujets d'attendrissement.
Pauvre ami, toi qui n'as pas
parlé depuis près de cinq ans,
toi qui as souffert tous les
martyres, comme tu es encore
vaillant et courageux. Tu es digne
de toutes les admirations et les
témoignages nombreux que je reçois
pour toi de la France et du
monde entier peuvent te prouver à
quel point tu es honoré et aimé.
Enfin quelques semaines encore et
nous tiendrons le bonheur. Pro-
fitant des journées de travail pour
toi, tu auras fort à faire de
te mettre au courant de tout ce
qui s'est passé, pour apprendre
à connaître les caractères des
hommes qui ont pris part à cette
terrible chose. Les uns sont bas
et vils et ne méritent que la
pitié, les autres sont des âmes
supérieures d'une pureté, d'une
élévation, d'un dévouement qui
font oublier beaucoup de vilaines
choses.

Letter from Lucie Dreyfus to Alfred Dreyfus, after their reunion in Rennes Prison
7 July 1899
Manuscript
Gift of the grandchildren of Captain Dreyfus
MAHJ 97.17.20

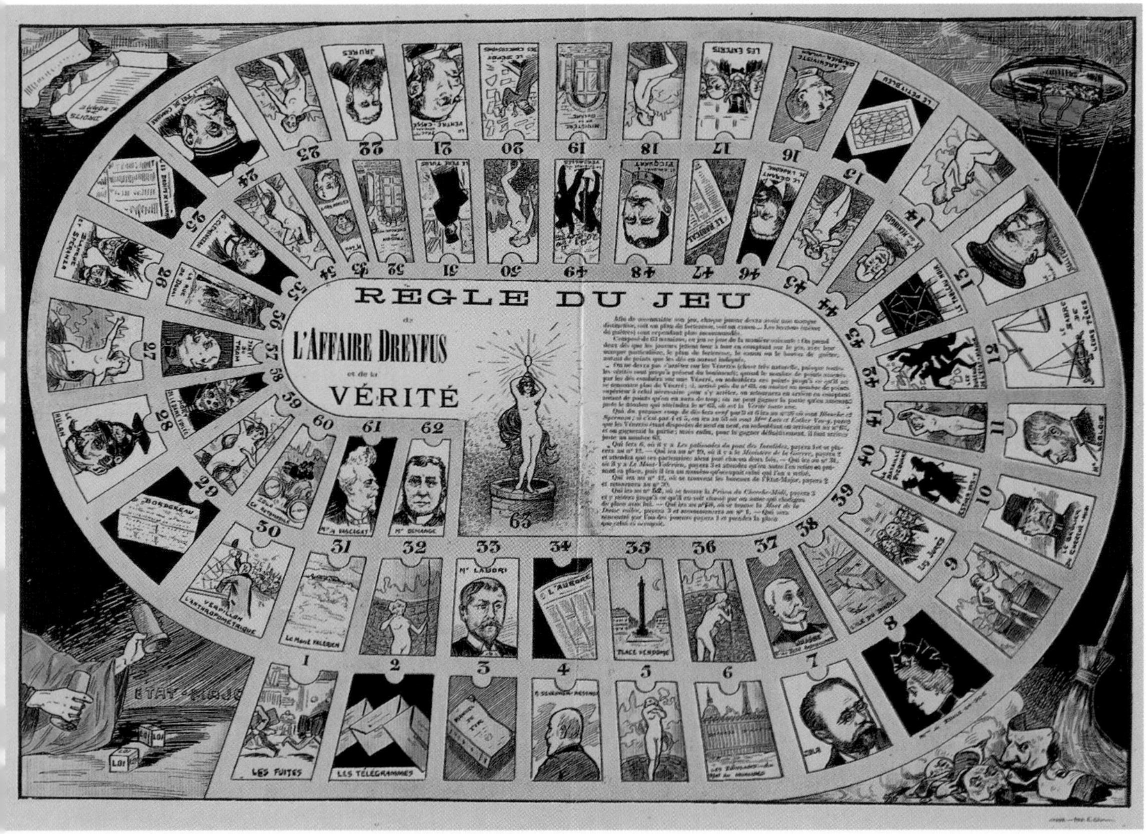

Dreyfus Affair
and Truth game

Sceaux, c. 1898
Poster
65 x 48 cm
Gift of Georges Aboucaya
in memory of
Colette Aboucaya-Spira
MAHJ 91.12.46

10 Political and intellectual movements in turn-of-the-century Europe

From the end of the eighteenth century, European Judaism entered into a phase of major upheavals, which increased in intensity until the middle of the twentieth century. They reflected economic, social, political and cultural changes taking place in Europe, where there was a growing tendency to have faith in reason, the only guarantee of political freedom, and in progress, both of individuals and of society as a whole. Traditional Judaism thus found itself being challenged by the descendants of the *Haskalah*.

On the religious front, the Reform movement, which began around 1810, gained momentum in Central Europe from the 1840s. It advocated a re-evaluation of ritual practices and the modernisation of the Synagogue service, so as to eradicate the more "separatist" aspects of it and to move closer, at least on the formal level, to the dominant religion. Reform synagogues were built in Seesen and Hamburg, where sermons were given in the language of the country by new-style rabbis, who, following the example of Abraham Geiger adapted the service to the mood of the times. Rabbinical seminaries were opened in Breslau, Budapest and elsewhere. There was a keen interest in exploring secular disciplines alongside Jewish studies.

In the intellectual field, the *Verein für Kultur und Wissenschaft des Judentums* (the Association for the Culture and Study of Judaism) was founded in Berlin, Germany, in 1821. The instigators came from traditional backgrounds, and included philosophers, such as Eduard Gans and Nahman Krochmal, and philologists, like Leopold Zunz, as well as men of letters including Heinrich Heine and rabbis Abraham Geiger and Zacharias Fraenkel. The establishment of Judaism as a subject of academic study removed from traditional exegesis seemed the only way to ensure both its modernisation and the recognition of its values by the outside world. Scientific societies and reviews proliferated in all the major Ashkenazi communities, creating a new perception of Jewish identity. Deriving directly from

Samuel Hirszenberg
(b. 1865, Lodz, d. 1908, Jerusalem)
Portrait of a Jewish Writer
1903
Oil on canvas
42.5 x 105 cm
MAHJ 93.12.1

the *Wissenschaft des Judentums*, modern Jewish history was born: between 1853 and 1876, Heinrich Graetz published his monumental History of the Jews: *Geschichte der Juden von den ältesten Zeiten bis auf die Gegenwart*. Despite the innovative character and scientific merits of his work, Graetz tended to underestimate the cultural richness of the communities of Eastern Europe.

From 1914, Simon Dubnow, (born in Mstislavl, Russia) who believed in secular nationalistic communal autonomy, worked on his World History of Jewish People: *Die Weltgeschichte des jüdischen Volkes*, 1925-30, which he continually tried to relate to the history of the surrounding societies. The historian was a founder member of YIVO, the Institute for Jewish Research, founded in Vilna in 1925.

Political ideologists burst on the Jewish scene at the end of the nineteenth century: the year 1897 saw both the birth of the Bund, the Jewish workers' party, and the first Zionist congress organised by Theodor Herzl in Basle. Some people joined the ranks of the revolutionaries, convinced that the fate of the Jews could only be improved by the overthrowing of the Tsarist regime and the advent of a new society in the Russian Empire.

The late nineteenth century also saw an explosion of ideas concerning Jewish languages. Often Russian-speaking, the Jewish intellectuals close to the Bund chose to speak and write in Yiddish, so as to be better understood by the people, which led to a reassertion of the Yiddish language, now considered as the vehicle for modern culture and political propaganda in Jewish circles. At the same time, highly talented writers, such as Mendele Moikher-Sforim, Sholem-Aleichem and Isaac-Leib Peretz won universal acclaim for Yiddish literature.

The emergence of Jewish national identity in Russia, in the 1880s, went hand in hand with the revival of Hebrew. Writers and poets such as Moses Leib Lilienblum, Ahad Ha'am and H̲ayyim Nah̲man Bialik were determined to resurrect and modernise Hebrew literature. The main architect in the reintroduction of Hebrew as a vernacular language was Eliezer ben Yehudah.

Theodor Herzl (b. 1860, Budapest, d. 1904, Edlach)

In Western Europe, emancipation had permitted the integration of the Jewish intellectual elites. Among them was Theodor Herzl, a law graduate, journalist and playwright. Herzl witnessed the election of the anti-Semitic mayor of Vienna, Karl Lueger, and Captain Dreyfus' public stripping of office, amid cries of "Death to the Jews!" His Zionist work was a reaction against anti-Semitism. In 1896, he wrote *Der Judenstaat*, (*The Jewish State*) and organised the first World Zionist Congress, the following year, in Basle, Switzerland. Convinced that only the establishment of a Jewish state, guaranteed by public law and international agreements, could save the Jews of Europe, Herzl, who did not specify the actual location of this Jewish state, placed the emphasis on the political and diplomatic aspect of its establishment. He founded the World Zionist Organisation, which produced a clash of different tendencies, and devoted his last years to defending the aim of a national Jewish homeland.

Boris Schatz
b. 1867, Varna, d. 1932, Denver)
Portrait of Herzl
Vienna, 1905
Bronze
40 x 28 cm
Gift of Theo Klein
MAHJ 96.52.13

Eliezer ben Yehudah
Postcard
Photograph: S. Narinsky,
published by Jamal Bros
Jerusalem, 1921
MAHJ cp/44.2

Eliezer ben Yehudah (1858-1922) and the revival of the Hebrew language

Between the end of the period of Mishnaic Hebrew (3rd century) and 1879, the year the first article by Ben Yehudah was published, Hebrew was used only as a scholarly language, and for prayer, but it was no longer spoken.

Eliezer ben Yehudah (Perelman), fought tirelessly to make Hebrew an accepted language of communication. He was supported by a network of teachers belonging to the Alliance Israélite Universelle in the training of a generation of Hebrew speakers. He compiled a monumental *Dictionary* and coined many new words and expressions. In 1890, Ben Yehudah set up the *Va'ad ha-lashon ha-'ivrit* (Council for the Hebrew language), bringing together linguists and writers. He borrowed from Arabic, but mostly he went back to the very early roots of Hebrew.

Modern Hebrew is a living language which is now evolving naturally, and whose spoken use has become richer and more diverse. This successful transition from a written to an oral form is unique in the history of the world's languages.

The Bund

The Bund (General Union of Jewish Workers in Lithuania, Poland, and Russia) was founded in Vilna in 1897. A Marxist-inspired party, it stemmed from the emergence of a large Jewish proletariat in the nineteenth century. Fiercely opposed to Zionism, Bundism advocated *doykeyt* – on the spot action, as opposed to aspiring to a future in another geographical place – and political autonomy in response to anti-Semitism in the Tsarist Empire. It promoted Yiddish as the Jewish national language.

Bund demonstration
1 May, Warsaw, 1924
Bund Archives/YIVO Institute
New York

Mendele Moikher Sforim
(1835-1917)
Isaac Leib Peretz
(1852-1915)
Sholem Aleichem
(1859-1916)
YIVO Institute, New York

The Yiddish language

Yiddish developed in the tenth century in the Rhine and Moselle valleys. It spread in successive waves until, by the beginning of the eighteenth century, it had become the vernacular language of all Ashkenazi Jews from Amsterdam to Venice, from Mulhouse to Riga. The *Haskalah* (Jewish Enlightenment), which influenced Western Europe in the eighteenth century, led to the decline of Yiddish. In Eastern Europe, the ideas of the *Haskalah* did not begin to spread until the nineteenth century. Despite a preference for Hebrew and Russian as the languages of culture, some writers chose to convey their social and cultural ideas in Yiddish. Yiddish was so deeply rooted in the population that, from the 1870s, a generation of intellectuals proclaimed it worthy of being the linguistic medium for a modern culture in the Jewish world.

Avant-garde reviews: *Yung Yiddish*

The review *Yung Yiddish* was founded in Lodz in 1919 by the poet Moyshe Broderzon and the artists Yankel Adler and Marek Szwarc. It was part of a general movement in modern art towards a synthesis of all the arts, later embodied by the reviews *Khalyastre* (Warsaw, 1922; Paris, 1924) and *Albatros* (Warsaw, 1922, Berlin, 1923). *Yung Yiddish* was innovative both in its content, which was a combination of poetry and avant-garde art, and for its design, printed on large sheets of wrapping paper. It published contributions from poets such as Yitzhak Katznelson and J.M. Neimann, and Yiddish writers from other cities, such as Moyshe Nadiv and Melekh Ravitch. It expanded its activities with the aim of forging links between Jewish and Polish writers and artists, and of organising exhibitions and public readings.

Marek Szwarc
(b. 1892, Zgierz, d. 1958, Paris)
Abraham and Hagar
Lodz, 1919
Woodcut on Japan paper
36.7 x 25.8 cm
MAHJ 97.16.10
Reproduced in *Yung Yiddish*
Lodz, 1919

Bezalel

In 1903, Boris Schatz, a Lithuanian-born sculptor with Zionist ideas, presented Theodor Herzl with a proposal for the establishment of a school of arts and crafts in Palestine. Its twin mandate was to foster a Jewish art rooted in the land of Israel and ancient Jewish history, and to create craft industries to improve the economic and social situation of the Jewish community, the *Yishuv*.

The project was adopted by the Seventh Jewish Congress held in Basle, and the school opened its doors in Jerusalem in February 1906. It bore the name of the first Hebrew craftsman, Bezalel Ben Uri Ben Hur, who had built the Tabernacle in the desert. From the outset, Bezalel included a museum that housed works of Jewish art, archaeological artefacts and collections of local flora and fauna, alongside the art school and studios where craftsmen of all ages produced objects from designs provided by the students.

The successive teachers at the school, Ephraim Moses Lilien, Samuel Hirszenberg, Ze'ev Raban, Abel Pann – all of whom were of European extraction – sought to provide Zionism with strong symbols drawn from the Bible and victorious episodes of Jewish history. The resulting Bezalel style reflected the meeting of Western art, especially Art Nouveau, and the imagery of a mythical Orient.

Ze'ev Raban's workshop
Bezalel school,
early 20th century
Gift of the Musée d'Art juif de Paris
MAHJ ph/113.740

Abel Pann
(b. 1883, Kreslawka,
d. 1963, Jerusalem)
The Creation of the World
Jerusalem, c. 1925
Colour lithograph
45.3 x 31 cm
MAHJ 94.17.1

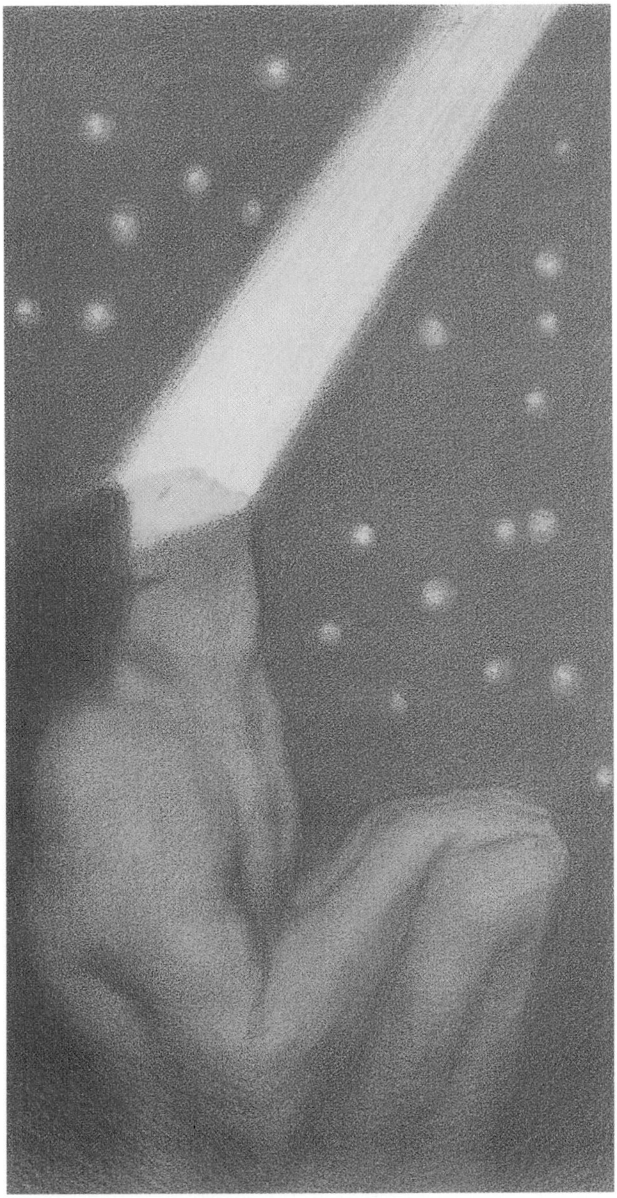

This colour lithograph, whose title is taken from Genesis 2:7: "...and breathed into his nostrils the breath of life", is part of a series of twenty-five plates illustrating "Genesis, from the Creation to the Flood". Abel Pann's work is clearly influenced by the Symbolists, in whose work Pann detected elements of mysticism, and French turn-of-the-century artists such as Puvis de Chavanne. His style changed radically when he moved to Jerusalem in 1920. He drew solely on Biblical themes. After Genesis, Pann embarked on the illustration of the Bible, a project which he did not complete. In a bid to break with Jewish diaspora identity, he abandoned the dramatic tones of the works of Russian and Polish artists and developed a documentary, almost ethnographic, approach to portraying Biblical heroes, drawing his inspiration from local communities.

The Jewish presence in twentieth-century art

11

The start of the twentieth century marked the culmination of Jewish reflection and artistic creation as an expression forged by specific cultural references. Judaism was moving towards upheaval, the social and cultural frameworks were disintegrating, and artists were confronted with the issue of their identity and modernity.

"The Jewish presence in twentieth-century art" is arranged in three sections, corresponding to three cities: St Petersburg, Berlin – where the notion of Jewish art developed – and Paris, the embodiment of emancipation for a generation that was moving away from the Jewish world.

El Lissitzky
(b. 1890, Potchinok,
d. 1941, Moscow)
Had Gadya
One only kid which my father bought for two zuzim
Kiev, Kultur Liege, 1919
Eleven lithographs on zinc
colour on paper
25.7 x 23.5 cm
Acquired with the support of the FRAM Ile-de-France and Claire Maratier
MAHJ 94.14.2

An unknown aspect of Lissitzky's work, the Yiddish prints and especially *Had Gadya*, with its use of the arch and the Hebrew letters as integral elements of the composition, emphasize the artist's development towards Constructivism. His choice of this traditional *Pesah* song for illustration, with its message of the existence of a supreme justice, suggests that he saw *Had Gadya* as an allegory for the victory of the Revolution.

St Petersburg

At the beginning of the twentieth century, in St Petersburg, a vast movement to recognise the Jewish cultural heritage was instigated with the founding of the Jewish History and Ethnography Society. In collaboration with the critic Stassoff, in 1905, Baron Horace Gunzburg published a large portfolio of Hebrew manuscripts from the St Petersburg library. This sparked off an interest in the Jewish ornamental tradition. The next stage in this reappropriation of a Jewish heritage was the organisation by An-sky of an ethnographic mission (1912-1915, then 1915-1916) to the Jewish Pale of Settlement, with the participation of artists such as Lissitzky, Rybak and Yudovine. From this encounter with Jewish folk and religious art, they tried to develop a specifically Jewish form of expression, combining tradition and the most recent developments in Western art, setting out down the path opened up by the Russian artists Larionov, Goncharova and Malevich who rediscovered folk imagery and the art of the icon. However, they very soon found this field of experimentation too restricted and abandoned it to pursue individual avenues.

Berlin

Around 1920, nearly 170,000 Jews lived in Berlin. Most of the Zionist Jewish organisations had their head offices there. Hebrew literature and the Hebrew press experienced an unprecedented boom, and the city became a hub of Jewish cultural revival. Berlin's artistic scene was dominated by the personality of Max Liebermann, president of the Berlin Acadamy of Fine Arts (1920-1933). The involvement of artists such as Joseph Budko, Ephraim Moses Lilien and Jakob Steinhardt in cultural Zionism, and their thinking on the issue of a national Jewish art stimulated the development of an original Jewish iconography, in which the treatment of Biblical themes bore the stamp of Art Nouveau and Expressionism. These artists formed the core of the Bezalel school in Jerusalem.

Paris

The term "Paris School" does not describe an artistic movement in the strict sense of the word, but a historic movement at the beginning of the twentieth century which propelled artists of all nationalities, including a high proportion of Jews, onto the Paris scene. With limited access to the artistic sphere in their native countries, these artists wanted to get to grips with modernity and become professional artists in complete freedom.

This sudden appearance of Jewish artists in a world where Jewish critics and art dealers were already prominent gave rise to the belief that there was a Jewish school. And yet, in their works, there is no identifiably Jewish theme; it is even difficult to find a common vocabulary or language. They were in Paris to paint, sculpt and absorb.

Many, like Lipchitz, Zadkine, Hayden, Marcoussis, Halicka and Sonia Delaunay embraced Cubism. There is also talk of "Jewish expressionism" in connection with the works of Soutine, Kikoine, Krémègne, Modigliani and even Pascin; an art form which supposedly combines a keen awareness of tradition (Rembrandt, Courbet, Chardin, and more recently, Cézanne and Van Gogh) and the melancholy, inner turmoil and existential angst specific to the Jews. Chagall is in a league of his own, appropriating the pictorial cultures of his time, taking inspiration from his own life and from an iconography that is both Russian and Jewish.

El Lissitzky
(b. 1890, Potchinok,
d. 1941, Moscow)
Moshe Broderzon (1890-1956)
Sihes Hulin
Moscow, 1916-1917
15 hand-coloured lithographs
25.3 x 31.7 cm
Acquired with the support
of the FRAM Ile-de-France
MAHJ 97.2.1

Sihes Hulin is the first testimony to the short and intense period of Jewish revival in Russia around 1910. Lissitzky and Broderzon, both involved in avant-garde movements, felt the need to combine newly-discovered tradition with a modernity they were trying to embrace. The story – a sixteenth-century tale whose hero is a rabbi adventurer – is inspired by the book of Jonah and old Yiddish literature, but the author develops a highly innovative style and rhyming system. The calligraphic text is by a *sofer* (scribe) on a scroll (a reference to the *Megillah*, the Scroll of Esther, which is read during the festival of *Purim*). The brightly coloured illustration depicts traditional Jewish motifs which Lissitzky had copied during his participation in the ethnographic mission in the Jewish Pale of Settlement.

According to Seth L. Wolitz, this title page summarises the intention of the work: a golden peacock, the symbol of Jewish artistic expression, is pulling a *Hasid* upwards: art is replacing religion as a source of spiritual exaltation. In the foreground, the poet, seeking inspiration, turns away from the scribe – who, on the right, holding the scroll, symbolises the past – and looks towards the artist depicted with his palette.
(Seth L. Wolitz, *Tradition and Revolution*, Jerusalem, 1987, p. 29).

Nathan Altman
(b. 1889, Vinnitsa,
d. 1970, Leningrad)
Evreiskaya Grafika
(words by Max Osborn)
St Petersburg, 1923
Ten lithographs in black
and with coloured borders
48.5 x 36.2 cm
Gift of Sally Kohn
Gift of the Musée d'Art juif
de Paris
MAHJ 2002.1.8

Born in Vinnitsa in Podolia, Nathan Altman studied in Odessa from 1903 to 1907. In 1910, he left for Paris. He attended Marie Vassilieff's Russian Academy, spent his days at the Louvre and moved into *La Ruche* ("The Beehive"), an artists' settlement on the edge of Montparnasse. On his return to Russia, he travelled to Gritsev, in Volhynia, in 1913, and discovered the richness of Jewish folk art through embroidered textiles in the synagogues and tombstones.
He recorded his impressions in a work entitled *Evreiskaya Grafika*, where his lithographs accompany a text on Jewish graphic art by Max Osborn. The deer, lions and doves, traditional motifs of Jewish iconography, can be seen in symmetrical black and white compositions made up of planes and Cubist-inspired distortions. Nathan Altman worked for the Revolution (he produced decorations for the first anniversary), at the same time carrying out his official duties within the Iso Narkompros, teaching and designing posters and stage sets (he created the sets for *The Dybbuk* and *Uriel da Costa* for the Habima Theatre).

Joseph Budko
(b. 1888, Plonsk, d. 1940, Jerusalem)
The Resurrection of the Dead
Tehiyyat ha-metim
Berlin, 1920
Black lead on paper
39 x 31 cm
MAHJ 95.10.1

After studying at the Vilna School of Fine Arts, Joseph Budko moved to Berlin in 1910, where he studied engraving with Hermann Struck. Taking Biblical themes as his inspiration, he devoted himself chiefly to the production and illustration of books. His *Haggadah* of 1917, with its effective interaction of text and illustration, represents a revival of the art of Jewish printing.
This drawing shows Ezekiel's prophecy in the Valley of the Dry Bones (Ezekiel 37:12: "I will open your graves and bring you up from them, and bring you to the land of Israel." It demonstrates Budko's ability to combine tradition, on which he drew, and the Zionist project, to which he was completely committed. In 1933, he emigrated to Palestine, where he was appointed director of the Bezalel "New School".

מוזגין לו כוס בני ותינוק שואל מה נשתנה

מה נשתנה הלילה הזה מכל־ הלילות שבכל־ הלילות אנו אוכלין

חמץ ומצה· הלילה הזה כלו מצה: שבכל־ הלילות אנו
אוכלין שאר ירקות הלילה הזה מרור: שבכל־ הלילות
אין אנו מטבילין אפילו פעם אחת· הלילה הזה שתי
פעמים: שבכל־ הלילות אנו אוכלין בין יושבין ובין מסבין.
הלילה הזה כלנו מסבין:

עבדים היינו לפרעה במצרים· ויוציאנו יי אלהינו משם
ביד חזקה
ובזרוע
נטויה.ואלו
לא הוציא
הקדוש
ברוך הוא
את אבותינו
ממצרים
הרי אנו
ובנינו ובני
בנינו
משעבדים היינו לפרעה במצרים· ואפילו כלנו חכמים· כלנו
נבונים· כלנו זקנים· כלנו יודעים את התורה· מצוה עלינו

Jacob Steinhardt
(b. 1887, Zerlow,
d. 1968, Jerusalem)
Haggadah shel Pesah
Berlin, 1922
Woodcut on Japan paper
38.5 x 29 cm
Gift of the Musée d'Art juif
de Paris
MAHJ 2002.1.10

Born in 1887 in Zerkow, Jacob Steinhardt trained in Berlin, where, in 1907, he was the pupil of Lovis Corinth and Hermann Struck. On returning from his travels to Italy and Paris, where he studied with Henri Matisse and Jean-Paul Laurens, he and Ludwig Meidner founded the *Pathetiker* group, and became associated with the poets' movement known as the *Neopathetiker*. After World War I, he took over Ephraim Moses Lilien's studio. Profoundly marked by the experience of the War, Steinhardt explored the themes of punishment and redemption, evident in his *Haggadah* of 1922. The twenty illustrations combine an intense expressionism – deformation of features, fragmentation of perspective – with a penetrating insight into the Jewish world of Eastern Europe. They introduce a psychological dimension into the scope of the traditional *Haggadah*. Franziska Baruch's layout and typography revive Hebrew printing to create one of its most remarkable achievements. In 1933, Steinhardt emigrated to Jerusalem, where he became a teacher and then the director of the Bezalel School of Fine Arts.

Moses Kisling
(b. 1891, Cracow,
d. 1953, Sanary-sur-Mer)
Nude
Paris, January 1918
Oil on canvas
54 x 81 cm
Gift of Alex Maguy
MAHJ 98.26.1

The son of a humble tailor who wanted him to be an engineer, Moses Kisling abandoned his studies to attend classes at the Cracow Academy of Fine Arts given by Josef Pankiewicz, a friend of Bonnard's and admirer of Renoir and Cézanne. It was Pankiewicz who inspired him to go to Paris to paint, and he settled there in 1910, at the age of nineteen. He soon met with success. He exhibited in Munich and Paris, at the Salon d'Automne and the Salon des Indépendants, thanks to his dealer, Basler. Kisling's studio, open to all, became one of the meeting places of Montparnasse. Until 1918, his work experimented with different styles.
This painting, contemporary with Modigliani's nudes, is very similar both in its composition, presenting the nude from behind and reducing it to a body and a mass of hair, and in its treatment of the background as a series of coloured planes, contrasting with the green of the curtain.

Ossip Zadkine
(b. 1890, Vitebsk, d. 1967, Paris)
Woman with Fan
Paris, 1920
Bronze
85 x 34 x 27 cm
On long-term loan from the Musée national d'Art moderne, Centre Georges Pompidou, Paris
D.98.6.19

Ossip Zadkine grew up in Smolensk, where his father, converted to Christianity on marrying the daughter of a Scottish family, taught Latin and Greek. In 1905, his family sent him to England to complete his studies, and he learned wood carving. In 1909, he was granted permission to enter France and he attended Injalbert's classes at the Paris École des Beaux Arts. From 1910 to 1912, he lived at *La Ruche* in relative isolation. He felt different from the other artists who worked there due to his education, but he did become very close to Modigliani. The output from his early years was influenced by Primitivism, and it was not until the early 1920s that he became interested in Cubism. He explored the theme of *Woman with a Fan* using various materials, stone, bronze and plaster. In this work, flat surfaces and convex areas combine in an interplay of light and shadow. The rounded forms of the thighs and breasts soften the sharper angles. A fan acts as a visual reference.

Marc Chagall
(b. 1887, Vitebsk, d. 1985,
Saint-Paul-de-Vence)
The Gates of the Cemetery
Vitebsk, 1917
Oil on canvas
87 x 68.5 cm
Gift of Ida Chagall, 1984
On long-term loan from the
Musée national d'Art moderne,
Centre Georges Pompidou, Paris
D.98.6.19

Marc Chagall was born in Vitebsk into a humble family – his father worked in a herring warehouse. He displayed a talent for art at a very early age. After a short apprenticeship with Yehudah Penn, a local master who trained a number of avant-garde artists, he studied under Leon Bakst in St Petersburg. In 1910, with the help of a grant awarded by a deputy of the Duma, he left for Paris, the "City of Light". His own painting was stimulated by the discovery of the museums, Cubism and the relations he developed with the poets Blaise Cendrars, Guillaume Apollinaire and André Salmon. He moved into *La Ruche*, exhibited at the Salon d'Automne and the Salon des Indépendants, from 1912 to 1914, and also in 1914 his works were shown by Herwarth Walden at the Berlin gallery Der Sturm. From there, he returned to Vitebsk, to join his fiancée Bella. The outbreak of war prevented him from going back to Paris. In 1917, he joined the Revolution, and echoed the hopes it brought for the Jews of Russia in this painting which combines the theme of the cemetery with that of resurrection.

1917 was also the date of the Balfour Declaration, promising the Jews a homeland. On the triangle over the gate, Chagall has inscribed the vision of the Prophet Ezekiel (Ezekiel 37:12-14). The letters on the tops of the gateposts: TKEB-TRN give the dates 1812-1890, possibly the dates on the tomb of his maternal grandfather which Chagall had just discovered, according to B. Harshav (*Marc Chagall, Les années russes, 1907-1922*, Paris, 1995).

Henri Hayden
(b. 1883, Warsaw, d. 1970, Paris)
Cubist composition
1917
Oil on canvas
97 x 65 cm
Gift of Claire Maratier
MAHJ 98.5.16

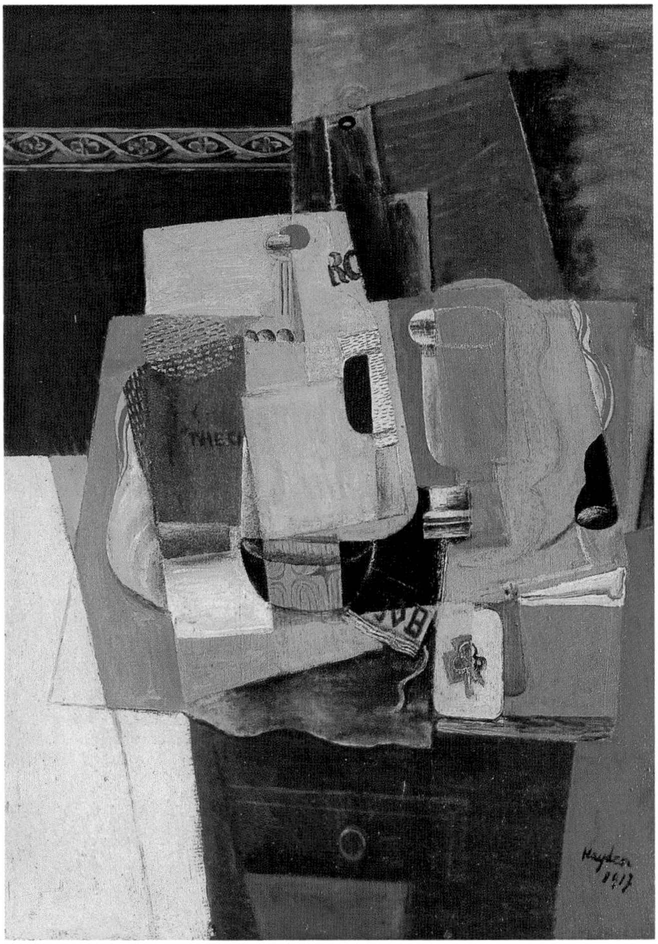

In 1905, Henri Hayden gave up studying to be an engineer and enrolled at the Warsaw School of Fine Arts. He left in 1907 and moved to Paris. Influenced initially by the Synthetism of the Pont-Aven School, he found in Cubism the answer to the search he had been engaged in since his arrival in France. It enabled him to reveal a new sensitivity, as shown in this still life, whose delicate colours and avoidance of rigid geometric forms convey a need for freedom which became more acute in 1922, when he broke away from Cubism.

Chana Orloff
(b. 1888, Tsara Konstantinovska,
d. 1968, Tel Aviv)
The Kiss, or The Family
Paris, 1916
Bronze
71.4 x 50.5 x 45.5 cm
Acquired through the generosity of the Justman-Tamir family
MAHJ 98.6.2

Chana Orloff is the only one of the artists of the Paris School to have spent her youth in Palestine, where her family, fleeing the Ukrainian pogroms, settled in 1904. In 1910, she left for Paris, where she was supposed to become a dressmaker. Her artistic vocation soon became apparent; she took classes at the *École des arts décoratifs*, and opted for sculpture. She soon became accepted into Paris artistic circles through her intense activity as a portraitist. Her sculpture was transformed by her meeting with Modigliani and her interest in Cubism. Her work became more radical, built of compact, simplified blocks.
The theme of the family and motherhood haunts Chana Orloff's work. Here the group is dominated by the hieratic figure of the father; the mother's face is reduced to the simplest form, just the arch of the eyebrows and the nose. The child is enveloped by the mother's body. The harmony of this intertwined group, the only one featuring a man, expresses a feeling of waiting and anguish.

Louis Marcoussis
(Ludwig Kasimir Markus)
b. 1878 Warsaw, d. 1941, Cusset
The Three Poets
Paris, 1929
Oil on canvas
162.5 x 130.5 cm
On long-term loan from the Musée national d'Art moderne, Centre Georges Pompidou, Paris
D.98.6.10

The son of a family of Warsaw industrialists, Marcoussis studied painting at the Academy of Fine Arts in Cracow. He and other artists and writers who were passionately interested in French culture were members of the Young Poland movement. He moved to Paris in 1903 and enrolled at the Académie Julian, where he became friends with Roger de La Fresnaye. Until 1907, he painted Impressionist canvases and participated in the Salon d'Automne and the Salon des Indépendants. In 1910, he met Braque and Apollinaire, who introduced him to Picasso. He embraced Cubism and exhibited at the Salon of the Section d'Or group. This canvas received acclaim when it was presented at the Bernheim Gallery, the year it was painted. It portrays three poets, the painter's closest friends: from top to bottom, André Salmon, Guillaume Apollinaire and Max Jacob. The outlines are drawn with a single, fluid line which evokes their common thinking and the bond between them.

Jacques Lipchitz
(Chaim Jacob)
b. 1891, Druskieniki,
d. 1973, Capri
Bather
1917-1919
Stone
107 x 37 x 38 cm
Gift of Ruben Lipchitz
MAHJ 93.10.7

Jacques Lipchitz used to say that a "miraculous" rabbi had predicted to his parents one day that their son would not be a rabbi, but would become somebody important among the Jews. His mother supported his wish to become a sculptor and to study in Paris, where he arrived in October 1909 at the age of eighteen. He enrolled at the École des Beaux-Arts and at the Académie Julian. His sculpture, rooted in the tradition of Maillol, began to develop from 1912. He was interested in Boccioni's sculpture, and became friends with Diego Rivera, Picasso and Duchamp-Villon, tackled Cubism, but did not produce his first truly Cubist works, beyond a simple stylistic effect, until 1915 (*Sailor with a Guitar*, Musée national d'Art moderne). His search soon led him towards abstraction. From 1917 to 1919 he produced a series of works entitled *Bather*, taking up the theme of the female anatomy again. This work is probably part of that series, although it is unfinished, which makes it hard to date.

Michel Kikoine
(b. 1892, Gomel, d. 1968, Paris)
The Little Bridge at Perrigny
1930
Oil on canvas
60 x 73 cm
Gift of Claire Maratier
MAHJ 98.5.4

Michel Kikoine's father, who worked in banking, accepted his son's vocation. The young artist spent his time at Jacob Krüger's private art school, in Minsk, where he met Chaim Soutine, and then left for Vilna, where he studied at the School of Fine Arts, at the same time as Pinchus Krémègne. He arrived in Paris in 1912, was a regular visitor at Cormon's studio and moved into *La Ruche* in 1914. At first, he painted post-Impressionist landscapes. His loyalty to the artists who had influenced his youth: Rembrandt, Courbet and Chardin, was unflagging, he always returned to his "masters", but it was in the discovery of the French landscape, in particular around his house in Annay-sur-Serein in Burgundy, that he really showed what he was capable of, and his painting came into its own. Here the artist achieved a totally personal synthesis between the Russian tradition of landscape painting, as embodied by Levitan, and Expressionism, the pictorial language he had forged during his years in Paris.

Chaim Soutine
(b. 1893, Smilovitchi, d. 1943, Paris)
Céret landscape
c. 1920
Oil on canvas
55 x 65 cm
Gift of Claire Maratier
MAHJ 98.5.12

Chaim Soutine was born into a poor family in a little village in Lithuania. His taste for painting, at odds with a traditional education, showed itself at a very early age. He left his family for Minsk, and then went to Vilna, where he studied at the School of Fine Arts.
He joined his fellow countrymen Kikoine and Krémègne in Paris, in 1913 and lived at *La Ruche* and the cité Falguière, where, like many others, he experienced poverty and deprivation.
In 1919, Léopold Zborowski, his dealer, sent him to the South of France. He stayed in the Roussillon, at Céret and in the Alpes-Maritimes, and at Cagnes.
During this period, his works displayed powerful colour, material and form. This landscape, typical of the Céret period, is constructed around a diagonal which makes the composition lean to the right.
Chaim Soutine painted relentlessly at Céret, but he destroyed many of his works from that period.

Pascin (Julius Pincus)
b. 1885, Viddin, Bulgaria,
d. 1930, Paris)

Alfred Flechtheim as a Toreador

Paris, 1925
Oil on canvas
104 x 80 cm
Alfred Flechtheim bequest, 1938
On long-term loan from the Musée national d'Art moderne, Centre Georges Pompidou, Paris
D.98.6.17

Pascin came from a Sephardi family in Bulgaria. After stays in Vienna, Berlin and Munich, where he worked on the satirical review *Simplicissimus*, he arrived in Paris in 1905, on Christmas Eve, where he was welcomed by a delegation from the Dôme café. He divided his time between Montmartre and Montparnasse, where he soon became a legendary figure. When war broke out in 1914, he decided to set sail for New York, where he had exhibited at the Armory Show in 1913. He spent the war years in the United States, and returned to Paris in 1920. During a visit to Paris by his friend, the German dealer Alfred Flechtheim, Pascin painted him dressed as a Toreador. His own taste for fancy dress was well known and during the sitting Pascin wore a bullfighter's costume. In a strange way, this costume epitomises the career of this brilliant, prodigious painter, who lived wildly, and took his own life for the love of a woman.

Pinchus Krémègne
(b. 1890, Zeludok,
d. 1981, Céret)
Woman sitting
Paris, c. 1930
Oil on canvas
81 x 60 cm
On long-term loan from
the Fondation
du Judaïsme français
D. 97.2.37

Born into a religious family who did not oppose his artistic vocation, Pinchus Krémègne studied sculpture at the Vilna School of Fine Arts, where he became friends with Chaim Soutine and Michel Kikoine. He left for Paris in 1912 and moved into *La Ruche*. From 1915, he concentrated on painting. His work, at first Symbolist, then Fauvist, developed very quietly, outside the main artistic movements, and was influenced both by Cézanne and Von Gogh. This portrait, which has the following inscription on the back :"Portrait of the mother of Soutine's daughter", is that of a young Polish girl, Deborah Melnik. Krémègne had her pose in a carefully arranged setting, where the model blends into the background dominated by blues, greens and mauves.

Gregory Michonze
(Michonznic)
b. 1902, Kishinev, d. 1982, Paris
On joue la rouge
(Let's try the red)
Paris, 1937
Oil on canvas
89.2 x 116.2 cm
On long-term loan from the Musée national d'Art moderne, Centre Georges Pompidou, Paris
D.98.6.20

After attending the School of Fine Arts in his home town, where he studied the technique of the icon, Gregory Michonze decided to leave for Paris, where he settled in 1922. He attended classes at the École des Beaux-Arts, and met Max Ernst, who introduced him into the Surrealist group. Until the beginning of the 1930s, he painted still lifes and surrealist compositions. He then moved away from Surrealism and opted for an art that he described as "surreal naturalism", which took shape from 1934 in large, very elaborate compositions preceded by an impressive number of studies. This work, originally entitled *Morning, On joue la rouge*, sums up Michonze's universe, where characters absorbed in their tasks, placed in rural landscapes surrounded by mysterious animals "look at each other without seeing each other, and live side by side without knowing each other". (Patrick Waldberg).

Jacques Lipchitz (Chaim Jacob)
b. 1891, Druskieniki, d. 1973, Capri
The Flight
Toulouse, 1940
Patinated plaster
37.2 x 37 x 22.2 cm
Gift of the Fondation Jacques et Yulla Lipchitz
On long-term loan from the Musée national d'Art moderne, Centre Georges Pompidou, Paris
D.98.6.9

Jacques Lipchitz's work rapidly developed from abstraction towards a lyrical expressionism. He adopted Biblical themes: *Jacob's struggle with the Angel, David and Goliath,* and his work took the direction of what he called "political sculpture".
His sculptures demonstrate his growing political awareness in the face of the rise of Nazism and the beginnings of the War. The monumental *Prometheus strangling the Vulture,* presented in Paris at the Exposition Universelle of 1937 exemplifies this development. Forced to flee Paris in May 1940, he took refuge in Toulouse, where he continued to draw and sculpt, and where he produced this piece, which represents the flight of a man, carrying a woman. When Lipchitz left for the United States in 1941, he took with him a portfolio and this sculpture in a bag.

SSIS Fres PELLETERIES
FANTS
MANUFACTURE DE CASQUETTES
J. S. JUDENSTEIN Fres
COMMISSION EXPORTATION
ESCALIER
C
CRAVATES

12

Being a Jew in Paris in 1939

The main courtyard of the Hôtel de Saint-Aignan
Paris, early 20th century
Photograph by the Seeberger brothers

The fate of the Hôtel de Saint-Aignan is typical of life in the Marais district, the *Pletzl* where Jews from Poland, Russia and Hungary gravitated from the beginning of the twentieth century.
There they rebuilt homes and a social fabric; they often set up family businesses in the clothing trade, cap-making, dressmaking, knitting or tie-making, or as watchmakers. They found a short-lived haven in Paris, until the legislation of the Vichy government either rounded them up or forced them to flee. On 16 July 1942, seven occupants of the Hôtel Saint-Aignan at 71 rue du Temple were arrested. In total, twelve people who lived there at the outbreak of World War II were deported and died.

The inhabitants of the Hôtel de Saint-Aignan in 1939

Located in a tiny inner courtyard which rises the whole height of the building, Christian Boltanski's installation, *The Inhabitants of the Hôtel de Saint-Aignan in 1939*, acts as a counterpoint to the décor and a poignant reminder of the grief associated with the building, a far cry from its glorious heyday, a piece of its missing history.

Christian Boltanski's work could be described as a kind of nominalism that seeks to restore a reality to people, things and sometimes gestures. Evoking literary works, including those of Georges Perec, and social, administrative or everyday practices, the work is made up of statements in affirmation of humanity in its uniqueness.

Even though Christian Boltanski has always refrained from dealing with the horrors of the Holocaust explicitly, or head on, all his work is underpinned the horror of death. *The Inhabitants of the Hôtel de Saint-Aignan in 1939* takes the form of the death notices that are posted on the walls of Eastern European cities. It is a work of great restraint and understatement, avoiding contrived emotion. Boltanski cites the names of the people who once lived in the building in the briefest way, giving only the surname, first name, place of birth, profession and sometimes a date. It is by this very omission that the gulf emerges between these ordinary people and those whose destiny History transformed into tragedy, gradually evoking the crime that caused that distinction. Installed in an abandoned space, this subtle monument, permanently there for all to see, pays tribute to those lives that were both unique and similar to so many others.

L.S.

Christian Boltanski
The inhabitants of the Hôtel de Saint-Aignan in 1939
Paris, 1998
Gift of the artist

ZUMAN WENDEZ
LAZARE ZOLTY
RAYMOND FRIEDMAN
ANNA SCHEIDECKER
MALKA HAGER
MORDKA ROSENCWEIG
SIMONE SCHILOVITZ
CHAJA SURA HAGER
PINKUS ZOLTY
POLOGNE
BELA ROSENCWEIG
MAURICE GAULON
NICOLE SCHILOVITZ
PARIS
COMPTABLE
GEORGES ROMA
MARGUERITE GOLLY
CÔTE-D'OR
COMPTABLE
LÉON LEIBOVICI
SEINE
GIFRA FRYDMAN
VARSOVIE
WOLF ROSENCWEIG
SEINE
ÉCOLIER
EMILE GOLLY
SEINE
WOLF BLUM FRYDLAND
NICOLAS REINER
BUDAPEST
BIJOUTIER
CHANA RO
JOSEPH MIRAMOND
HÉRAULT
ADÈLE DROU
LOIRET
FANNY ROSENCWEIG
SEINE
ÉCOLIÈRE
PAULA KRAEMER
GRODNO
CONFECTION POUR DAMES
27 JUILLET 1942
JACQUES
MYRIAM ZOLTY
VARSOVIE
LUCIE DUGAN
SEINE
BLANCHISSEUSE
HUGUETTE ROSENCWEIG
SEINE
ÉCOLIÈRE
YEHIEL BER ZOLTY
POLOGNE
BONNETIER
ANGÈLE SCHEIDECKER
SEINE
GEORGES SCHILOVITZ
VARSOVIE
MAROQUINIER
MARKIEL ROTHSTEIN
KOZEWA
MANŒUVRE
25 JUIN 1941
ALBERT FA
SEINE
CHAUFFEUR DE
JEANNE KERSCHENBAUM
PARIS
EMPLOYÉE DE L'OFFICE CENTRAL DE PHARMACIE
LOUISE ROMAIN
CHARENTE
COUTURIÈRE

"Early yesterday morning, foreign Jews were requested by police officers to board buses. They left for a new destination, presumably to work." *France-Soir*

The Vélodrome d'Hiver round-up

The buses parked along the façade, rue Nélaton, 15th *arrondissement,* Paris 16-17 July 1942 Bibliothèque historique de la Ville de Paris

---

According to Raul Hillberg, 5,000,200 Jews perished in the Holocaust, including 70,000 French Jews. (*La destruction des juifs d'Europe*, Fayard, 1988, p. 1046.)

The Holocaust
Chronology

1933

30 January
Adolf Hitler becomes Chancellor of the Reich. After dissolving the Reichstag, he embarks on the elimination of all opponents to the regime.

20 March
Official announcement of the opening of the concentration camp at Dachau, to hold 5,000 political prisoners detained "for the public good". These include Jewish prisoners arrested for their political or trade union activities.

23 March
Hitler grants himself full powers for four years, signalling the end of democracy in Germany.

1 April
The first anti-Jewish measures in Germany, with the organisation of a four-day boycott of Jewish shops. Throughout April, a series of "Aryan laws" are passed, such as the exclusion of Jews from public service and the bar, and the introduction of *numerus clausus* restricting access to universities.

May
First book-burnings of works by Jews.

1934

2 August
After the death of Marshal Hindenburg, Hitler combines the posts of Chancellor and President of the Reich.

19 August
The overwhelming majority of German citizens vote yes in the referendum, approving this decision. Hitler is now *Reichsführer*.

1935

15 September
Promulgation of the Nuremberg laws, supposedly to protect German blood and honour. These laws, based on so-called racial criteria, excludes Jews from German society.

1938

March
Annexation of Austria (*Anschluss*). Adolf Eichmann opens a Jewish Emigration Centre in Vienna to organise the mass departure of the Jews from Austria. The Jews of Germany are also driven out so that the Reich can quickly be *Judenrein* (purged of Jews).

10 November
"Night of Broken Glass" (*Kristallnacht*). Attacks on individuals, synagogues destroyed, looting of Jewish shops. The Jewish community of Germany is ordered to pay compensation of one billion marks for causing this damage by provoking the "justifiable anger of the German people."

End November
New German edicts banning Jews from public places and excluding Jewish children from schools.

1939

January
Establishment of a Central Bureau for Jewish Emigration in Berlin. The Nazi authorities implement a dual policy of segregation and expulsion.

30 January
Hitler addresses the Reichstag: "Europe will not find peace until the Jewish race has been eradicated from Europe."

1 September
Expulsion of the Jews living in mainly German-speaking regions of Poland, and compulsory relocation of those living in rural areas to the cities.

October
Beginning of random deportation of the Jews to the Lublin area, where the Nazi authorities plan to build a "Jewish reservation". The same month, in Germany, start of the euthanasia policy for the mentally ill, or Operation 14.

23 November
Compulsory special badge for the Jews of Poland, a white armband with a blue Star of David.

December
Beginning of the census of the Jews of Poland, who are now prohibited from moving around.

Winter
Beginning of the "ghettoisation" process.

1940

April
Establishment of the Lodz ghetto.

May
Building works begin on the Auschwitz I camp, designed to be a concentration camp.

27 September
First German edict imposing a census of Jews in the occupied zone.

3 October
1st Jewish statute promulgated by the Vichy government, banning the Jews from certain professions.

4 October
Vichy Law giving Prefects the power to intern "foreigners of the Jewish race" in "special camps".

7 October
Repeal of the Crémieux Decree of 1870 which had enfranchised the Jews of Algeria.

October
Establishment of the Warsaw Ghetto.

1941

29 March
Setting up of the Office for Jewish Affairs, to ensure the application of the Pétain government's anti-Jewish policies.

14 May
First mass arrest of Jews in Paris. Internment in the Pithiviers and Beaune-la-Rolande camps.

2 June
Promulgation of the 2nd Jewish statute, increasing exclusion.

22 June
Germany invades the Soviet Union as part of the Barabarossa operation. *Einsatzgruppen* (special mobile units) follow the regular troops, massacring entire communities as they advance.

End June
Auschwitz extension works begun.

22 July
Beginning of the "Aryanisation of Jewish property", which strips French Jews of their belongings.

31 July
Note from Goering to Heydrich asking him to embark on preparations for the "Final Solution to the Jewish question".

20-25 August
Round-up in the 11th arrondissement of Paris. The French and foreign Jews arrested are interned in the Drancy camp.

18 September
Letter from Himmler announcing Hitler's decision to deport all the Jews "eastwards" from territory subject to the Reich.

20 September
Building of the Auschwitz-Birkenau extermination camp, and, within a few days, the opening of Lublin-Majdanek camp.

21 September
German edict making it compulsory for all Jews over the age of six to wear the yellow star.

Mid-October
Beginning of deportation of Jews from the Reich: 20,000 people transferred to the Lodz Ghetto.

23 October
Jewish emigration banned.

Autumn
Beginning of mass gassing of Jews with exhaust fumes from diesel lorries.

October-November
Building of two concentration camps in Poland, Belzec and Chelmno, then of the extermination machinery at Treblinka camp.

8 December
First gas chamber exterminations at Chelmno.

12 December
Several hundred French Jews arrested in Paris, including numerous leading political and cultural figures. They are interned in the Compiègne-Royallieu camp.

1942

2 January
Decree ordering a census of all Jews who have settled in France since 1936 and are residing in the free zone.

20 January
Wannsee conference: SS leaders meet in conditions of great secrecy to work out the practical details for implementing the "Final Solution".

February
Beginning of mass gassings at Auschwitz-Birkenau.

Early March
Opening of Belzec extermination camp.

March
Beginning of mass deportation of Polish Jews to the extermination camps. Within a few months, the ghettos are virtually emptied of their populations.

22 March
Departure of the first deportation convoy from France, which left Drancy heading "eastwards".

March-June
Deportation of the Jews of Slovakia, Bessarabia and Bukovina.

April
Opening of Sobibor extermination camp.

29 May
Compulsory wearing of the yellow star for all Jews over the age of six in the occupied zone.

25 June
Beginning of negotiations between French government representatives (Bousquet, Leguay) and German leadership to organise the arrest and deportation of French Jews. The question of children under the age of sixteen arises, and Pierre Laval decides to include them in the deportation convoys.

16 July
Vélodrome d'Hiver round-up.
Nearly 13,000 foreign Jews interned at Drancy, including women and children for the first time.

July
Beginning of mass gassings at Treblinka.

August
First week: transfer of several thousand foreign Jews interned in camps in the southern zone to the occupied zone; they are subsequently deported.
Deportation of the Jews of Croatia.

26 August
Major round-up of foreign Jews throughout the unoccupied zone.

11 November
German occupation of the southern zone. French Jews find themselves trapped.

December
Order for all the Tziganes of the Reich to be deported to Auschwitz.

1943

22-27 January
Major round-up of Jews in Marseille during the destruction of the Old Port area.

March-May
Deportation of the Jews of Thrace and Macedonia (recently integrated with Bulgaria) and of the Jews of Greece.

19 April – 16 May
Warsaw Ghetto uprising.

September
First arrests of Jews in the Italian zone.

Autumn
Deportation of the Italian Jews.

1944

May-July
Deportation of the Hungarian Jews

Spring-summer
"Death marches" of the prisoners from the Polish camps to the camps of Central Europe as the Nazis try to flee the advance of the Allied Forces.

31 July
Departure of the last deportation convoy of French Jews.

9 August
Decree from the interim government of France nullifying all the laws and acts of discrimination against the Jews.

17 August
The last train leaves Drancy for Buchenwald. Twenty-five people manage to escape on the night of 20 August.

1945

January
Arrival of Soviet troops at Auschwitz-Birkenau.

May
Opening of the gates of Mauthausen.

November
Beginning of the Nuremberg trials.

13 The Contemporary Jewish World

Five photographers from the Magnum Photo Agency portray the postwar Jewish communities of Israel, France, the former USSR and the United States.

Robert Capa
A Jew of Hungarian origin, Robert Capa fled Nazi Germany in 1933 and settled in Paris. His reportage of the Spanish Civil War in 1938 earned him international fame. He emigrated to the United States. As a correspondent for *Life* magazine, he photographed World War II and accompanied John Steinbeck to the USSR. He was one of the founders of the Magnum Agency, in 1947. From 1948 to 1950, he spent long periods in Israel and photographed the beginnings of the new state. In 1954, he was killed by a mine in Thai-Bin, Vietnam.

Immigrants arriving at Haifa by boat, 1948
MAHJ 99.43.9

Since the beginning of the modern era, the Jewish world has undergone profound upheavals, which have affected both its consciousness of itself and its relations with the surrounding society. Between 1941 and 1945, European Judaism was crushed by Nazi persecution and, still today, the Holocaust remains part of Jewish consciousness as a defining event in the history of humanity. Since 1948, the Jews have once more had a homeland, and founded a state: Israel.

Nowadays, a quarter of the thirteen million Jews worldwide live in Israel. The country has seen successive waves of immigration, from Russia, Poland, Romania, Germany and other Western European countries, from the Islamic countries, from America, as well as two influxes from the former Soviet Union and Ethiopia in the 1980s. Israel continues to fulfil the objective defined by the Zionist ideologists: the ingathering of the exiles, *kibbutz galuyot*.

Seventy one percent of the Jews of the diaspora (around eight million) live in America, mainly in North America. Well integrated into the melting-pot, the American Jewish community is vital and active, divided into several religious groupings, from orthodox to liberal Judaism.

The biggest Jewish communities in Western Europe are those of France and Great Britain. French Jews have remained profoundly influenced by the message of emancipation and, while remaining faithful to their roots, have demonstrated an steadfast attachment to the values of the Republic. Over the last fifteen years, there has been a revival of religious practice.

In the Communist countries, the Jewish communities that survived the Holocaust had to conceal their differences for nearly fifty years, accused of "chauvinism" by the authorities. The collapse of Communism permitted the revival of small groups and the emergence of a new questioning of Jewish identity among Jews from

Patrick Zachmann
Born in 1955 at Choisy-le-Roi, Patrick Zachmann joined the Magnum Agency in 1985. Over seven years, he combined work on a project on the integration of young immigrants in Marseille, with a private survey on Jewish identity in France. More recently, he has been photographing the Chinese diaspora.

Celebrating the thirty-third birthday of the State of Israel, Salle Gaveau, Paris, March 1981
MAHJ 99.43.30

Eastern Europe often anxious to rebuild links with their historical and cultural roots, but without belonging to a strictly religious definition (complicated by the very high number of mixed marriages).

Decolonisation, and the subsequent anti-Jewish campaigns linked to the creation of the State of Israel and latterly to the successive Arab-Israeli wars that have taken place since 1948, have led to the disappearance of the once large and thriving Jewish communities of North Africa. Their members emigrated to Israel, Western Europe – mainly France – Canada and South America. South Africa has a fairly large Jewish community (nearly 120,000), as does Australia, (around 90,000).

Contemporary Judaism is characterised by both a religious revival – part of a general trend – on the one hand, and increasing integration verging on assimilation, on the other. There is a conflict between traditional values embodied in structured communities, and insistence on the possibility of different expressions of Jewish identity.

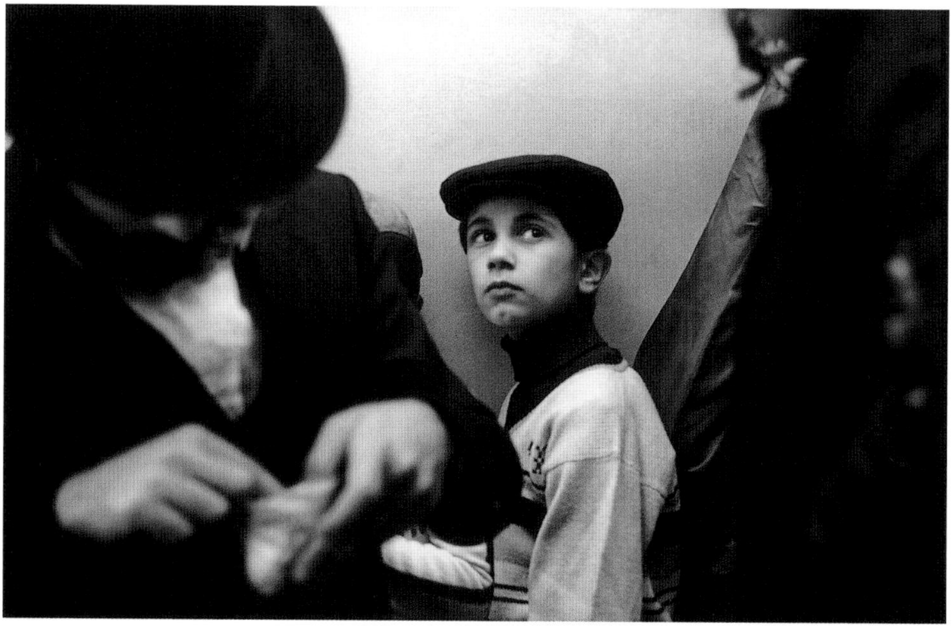

Gyorgy Pinkhassov
Born in Moscow in 1952, Russian, naturalised French. After studying film and working as a cameraman at the Mosfilm studios, Pinkhassov moved to Paris in 1985, where he finally opted for photography. This series on the Jews of Uzbekistan, photographed in 1988, shows the influence of his cinema background.

Tashkent, Uzbekistan, 1988
MAHJ 99.43.24

Micha Bar-Am

Born in 1930, in Berlin, Micha Bar-Am grew up in Haifa. He became a photographer during the Sinai campaign in 1956. For the next nine years he worked for the Israeli Army review, *ba-Mahaneh*. He subsequently became a correspondent for the *New York Times*, and still follows Israeli news.

Watermelon vendor in Tel Aviv, 1974
MAHJ 99.43.3

Leonard Freed
Born in New York in 1929, of Russian-Jewish parents. His photographs of orthodox Jews in the United States, France and Britain show his fascination with orthodox Jewish communities. He is convinced that they are the "source of the constantly renewed energy of Judaism and its revival". "My mother came from a *shtetl*, a Jewish village in Eastern Europe. She used to say: 'You can take a Jew out of *shtetl*, but you can't take the *shtetl* out of the Jew.' Outside the *shtetl* the Jews prospered, and, with money, came sartorial elegance, although the men continued to wear black, the sign of humility. I wondered why so few men wore a tie. I was told that there was no need if they wore a beard." But most of the students have very little facial hair. 'Oh, they'd reply, but they'll get there.'" (*La danse des fidèles*, Le Chêne, Paris, 1984).

United States, 1954
MAHJ 99.43.20

Musée d'art et d'histoire du Judaïsme

Board of directors

Théo Klein, *Chairman*
Claude-Gérard Marcus, *Honorary Chairman*
Christophe Girard, *Deputy Mayor of Paris in charge of culture, Vice-Chairman*
Francine Mariani-Ducray, *Director of the Musées de France, Vice-Chairman*

Moïse Cohen, *President of the Consistoire israélite de Paris*
Nelly Hansson, *Director of the Fondation du Judaïsme français*
Viviane Huchard, *Chief Heritage Curator, Director of the Musée national du Moyen Âge*
Philippe Kraemer, *representative of the Musée d'Art juif de Paris*

Pierre Aidenbaum, *Mayor of the 3rd arrondissement*
Dominique Bertinotti, *Mayor of the 4th arrondissement*
Michel Clément, *Director of Architecture and Heritage*
Hélène Font, *Director of Cultural Affairs of the City of Paris*
Anne Hidalgo, *first Deputy Mayor of Paris*
Victor Klagsbald, *representative of the Musée d'Art juif de Paris*
David de Rothschild, *President of the Fonds social juif unifié*
Eric Schieber, *representative of the Musée d'Art juif de Paris*
Dominique Viéville, *Head of the Inspection générale des musées*
Jean-Jacques Wahl, *Director of the Alliance Israélite Universelle*
Anita Weber, *Regional Director of Cultural Affairs, Île-de-France*
A representative of the Central Consistory

Scientific Committee

Christian Boltanski
Georges Brunel, *Chief Heritage Curator*
Isac Chiva, *Honorary Director of Studies at the EHESS*
Michel Garel, *Chief Curator, Department of Oriental Manuscripts, Bibliothèque nationale de France*
André Kaspi, *Professor at the University of Paris I*
Norman Kleeblatt, *Curator at the Jewish Museum, New York*
Maurice Kriegel, *Director of Studies at the EHESS*
Gérard Nahon, *Director of Studies at the EPHE*
Dominique Ponnau, *Honorary Director of the École du Louvre*

Members of the committee until 1998:
Zeev Gourarier, Victor Klagsbald,
Judith Meyer-Petit, Edward Van Voolen.

The Guide

Authors

Laurence Sigal-Klagsbald

Anne Grynberg for the Introductory texts,
except for chapters 1, 4, 6, and 11
and for the Chronology of the Holocaust.
Nathalie Hazan-Brunet
Anne Hélène Hoog

Contributors

Juliette Braillon-Philippe
(The Jewish presence in twentieth-century art)
Daniela Nittenberg (pp. 93, 128, 129, 130);
Dorota Sniezek-Feijoo (pp. 89-90, 92);
Ami Bouganim (p. 63), Sophie Kessler-Mesguich (pp. 29, 118);
Victor Klagsbald (p. 54), Evelyne Oliel-Grausz (p. 31);
Gilles Rozier (pp. 119-120); Joël Touati (pp. 80, 82).

Editor

Nathalie Hazan-Brunet
Assisted by Juliette Braillon-Philippe

Picture Researcher

Nicolas Feuillie

Edited by

Lucilia Jeangeot

English Translation

Ros Schwartz

Edited by

Alisa Jaffa

Graphic Design

Compagnie Bernard Baissait,
Bernard Lagacé

Photoengraving

Blanchard Printing

Photographic credits

Micha Bar-Am, Magnum Photos: p. 156
Gilles Berizzi, Réunion des musées nationaux, Paris:
p. 20; 22, 25, 26, 29, 32, 33, 36, 38, 39, 41, 42, 43,
44, 47, 50, 51 (bottom), 52, 53 (centre),
59, 65, 71, 74, 75, 76, 76, 77, 78, 79, 80, 81, 82,
83, 86, 87, 88, 89, 92, 93, 98, 99, 100 (bottom),
103, 106, 107, 108 (bottom), 109, 113, 114, 117, 135.
BHVP, Fonds France-Soir: p. 148
Caisse nationale des monuments historiques: Paris, p. 144
Robert Capa, Magnum Photos: p. 152
Gérard Dufrêne, Musée d'art et d'histoire
du Judaïsme, Paris: p. 66
Nicolas Feuillie, Musée d'art et d'histoire du Judaïsme,
Paris: p. 4, 48, 54, 55, 62, 70, 94, 102, 112, 118, 121, 127, 128
Flammarion, Paris: p. 12
Christophe Fouin,
Direction des Affaires culturelles, Paris: p. 14, 17
Leonard Freed, Magnum Photos: p. 157
Mario Goldman, Musée d'art et d'histoire du Judaïsme,
Paris: p. 19, 24, 51 (top, centre), 53 (top, bottom), 58, 61,
67, 91, 97, 105, 108 (top), 111, 123, 129, 130
Daniel Laclef, Musée d'art et d'histoire
du Judaïsme, Paris: p. 64
Jacques L'Hoir, Musée d'art et d'histoire
du Judaïsme, Paris: p. 73, 137
Musée d'art et d'histoire du Judaïsme,
Paris: p. 11, 68, 84, 110, 122
Musée national d'art moderne,
Centre Georges-Pompidou, Paris:
p. 132, 133, 136, 140, 142, 143
Orlando photo, Musée d'art et d'histoire
du Judaïsme, Paris: p. 23
Percheron, Artephot: p. 7
Gueorgui Pinkhassov, Magnum Photos: p. 155
Réunion des musées nationaux, Paris: p. 37
Adam Rzepka, Musée d'art et d'histoire
du Judaïsme, Paris: p. 30, 40, 56, 72, 90, 101, 124, 147
Succession Abel Pann: p. 123
ND-Viollet: p. 13
Yivo Institute for Jewish Research, New York: p. 119, 120
Patrick Zachmann, Magnum Photos: p. 154
DR.: p. 34

Cover

Hand-shaped pointed, *yad*

Galicia, c. 1800.

Strauss Collection, Rothschild donation. On long-term loan from the Musée national du Moyen Âge, Paris,

CL. 12264.

Inside front cover

The main courtyard of the Hôtel de Saint-Aignan

Paris, early 20th century

Photo: Seeberger Brothers

Printed in May 2003
Blanchard Printing, Le Plessis-Robinson.

Dépôt légal:
August 1999 for the first English edition and
May 2003 for the second English edition - no. P1898
ISBN : 2-913391-02-8